THE INNER LIFE OF *MRS. DALLOWAY*

LEONARD HASTINGS SCHOFF
MEMORIAL LECTURES

UNIVERSITY SEMINARS
LEONARD HASTINGS SCHOFF
MEMORIAL LECTURES

The University Seminars at Columbia University sponsor an annual series of lectures, with the support of the Leonard Hastings Schoff and Suzanne Levick Schoff Memorial Fund. A member of the Columbia faculty is invited to deliver before a general audience three lectures on a topic of his or her choosing. Columbia University Press publishes the lectures.

Robert Gooding-Williams, *Democracy and Beauty: The Political Aesthetics of W. E. B. Du Bois*

Robert G. O'Meally, *Antagonistic Cooperation: Jazz, Collage, Fiction, and the Shaping of African American Culture*

Herbert S. Terrace, *Why Chimpanzees Can't Learn Language and Only Humans Can*

Annette Insdorf, *Cinematic Overtures: How to Read Opening Scenes*

Paige West, *Dispossession and the Environment: Rhetoric and Inequality in Papua New Guinea*

Robert L. Belknap, *Plots*

Philip Kitcher, *Deaths in Venice: The Cases of Gustav von Aschenbach*

Douglas A. Chalmers, *Reforming Democracies: Six Facts About Politics That Demand a New Agenda*

Boris Gasparov, *Beyond Pure Reason: Ferdinand de Saussure's Philosophy of Language and Its Early Romantic Antecedents*

Robert W. Hanning, *Serious Play: Desire and Authority in the Poetry of Ovid, Chaucer, and Ariosto*

For a complete list of books in the series, please see the Columbia University Press website.

THE INNER LIFE OF *MRS. DALLOWAY*

EDWARD MENDELSON

Columbia University Press   *New York*

Columbia University Press
Publishers Since 1893
New York   Chichester, West Sussex

Copyright © 2025 Columbia University Press
All rights reserved

Library of Congress Cataloging-in-Publication Data
Names: Mendelson, Edward, author.
Title: The inner life of Mrs. Dalloway / Edward Mendelson.
Description: New York : Columbia University Press, 2025. |
Series: Leonard Hastings Schoff memorial lectures | Includes index.
Identifiers: LCCN 2025008748 (print) | LCCN 2025008749 (ebook) |
ISBN 9780231221702 hardback | ISBN 9780231221719 trade paperback |
ISBN 9780231563864 ebook
Subjects: LCSH: Woolf, Virginia, 1882–1941. Mrs. Dalloway |
LCGFT: Literary criticism
Classification: LCC PR6045.O72 M7359 2025 (print) |
LCC PR6045.O72 (ebook) | DDC 823/.912—dc23/eng/20250324

Cover design: Julia Kushnirsky

GPSR Authorized Representative: Easy Access System Europe,
Mustamäe tee 50, 10621 Tallinn, Estonia, gpsr.requests@easproject.com

For Barbara J. Fields

CONTENTS

Preface ix

Introduction: Two Quests and a Sacrifice 1

1 Medicine 25

2 Empire 51

3 Love 81

Epilogue: The Afterlife of the Text 105

Acknowledgments 129
Reference Notes 131
Index 135

PREFACE

Mrs. *Dalloway* is a book about almost everything: love and hate, peace and war, mind and body, sleep and waking, youth and age, health and disease, nature and civilization; about food, sex, money, status, power, freedom, language, psychology, technology, history, justice, and much else. Virginia Woolf wrote in her diary: "I want to give life and death, sanity and insanity; I want to criticize the social system, and to show it at work, at its most intense." No book about *Mrs. Dalloway* can respond to more than a few fractions of it. This book expands on three talks about the novel, each focusing on one of its many themes, that I gave at Columbia University a few years ago, in the Leonard Hastings Schoff Memorial Lectures Series. I have tried to give some sense of the immense depth and breadth of the novel, knowing how partial this triple-themed account must be.

The Hogarth Press, owned and founded by Leonard and Virginia Woolf, published *Mrs. Dalloway* a century ago, in 1925. I have been thinking and writing about it for more than half that century. In addition to the three talks that are at the center of this book, I have adapted, in my introduction and epilogue, much of an essay that I wrote in 2022 for the *New York Review of Books* about two new editions of the novel. I have not looked back at the chapter that I wrote about the novel twenty years ago for a book called *The Things That Matter*, but I have inevitably repeated some of its points. I have frequently quoted W. H. Auden, not only because I have written extensively about him elsewhere, but because he understood human beings in much the same way that Virginia Woolf did, and shared her passionate commitment to the value of unique personal selves. Each illuminates the other in ways that no one else can match.

While writing about some of the pervasive themes in *Mrs. Dalloway* I began to sense, with something close to awe, the density and depth of the connections that Virginia Woolf had woven into it. Medicine, empire, and love—the themes of my three central chapters—provided her with some of the materials that she brought together into a coherent whole, but her network of connections extends far beyond those themes. Almost every detail in the book echoes or counterpoints dozens of other details in ways that a reader may notice only after many readings. A summary of the plot would say nothing about, for example, brothers and sisters, but siblings and their relations are everywhere in the texture of the prose. Having written chapters about medicine, empire, and love, I can imagine further chapters on, for another example, clothing: Miss Kilman in her mackintosh, Clarissa mending her dress early in the book and her later sense of her party's splendor falling to the floor, "so strange it was to come in alone in her finery." Or on flowers: from the flowers that she said she would buy herself, through Hugh Whitbread's carnations that Lady Bruton suddenly stuffs into her dress, to the roses that Richard Dalloway presents in silent embarrassment to Clarissa, and dozens more.

Each of these themes tells a story that forms a counterpoint to the central plot, somewhat in the way that the inner voices of

Bach's four-part fugues act as counterpoints to the outer melody. A composer once advised his students that, if they couldn't come up with a melody that they had been commissioned to write, they could borrow one of those inner voices from Bach: it would make a better melody than anything they could have written on their own, and no one would guess where it came from. All of Virginia Woolf's novels have networks of meaning like the ones in *Mrs. Dalloway*, but each is built up from a different set of themes, a different set of inner voices and invisibly connected incidents. The only other writer in English with the same kind of thematic and connective powers seems to be Shakespeare.

A word about texts. I have quoted from the 1929 third impression of the 1925 first edition published by the Hogarth Press. The 1929 printing includes nine minor changes that Virginia Woolf made after the first printing appeared; it is the only text that she supervised and revised, and, except for a few typing and proofreading errors and one word miscorrected by the printer, comes closer than any other to what she expected to see on the page. (Searchable images of this and other early editions may be found at https://mendelson.org/VirginiaWoolf.) All later texts are marred by printers' errors or adulterated by well-meaning editors who, to varying degrees, both reject the author's changes and impose needless changes of their own.

All current editions are imperfect, but the Penguin Classics version edited by Stella McNichol, published in Britain in 1992 and elegantly reset for an American edition in 2021, seems to me the most useful and reliable among the many editions that include explanatory notes and an introductory guide to interpretation. My epilogue says a few things about the subtle but significantly different ways in which different editions distort the novel that Leonard and Virginia Woolf published as a plain text without an introduction or notes. A new edition that avoids, I hope, the textual faults of earlier ones, and is uninterrupted by endnote numbers, will be published by New York Review Books around the same time that the present book appears.

A word about names. This book uses the full name "Virginia Woolf," never a shorter form; Hermione Lee's great biography does the same. Virginia Woolf, in her diary and letters, typically called herself "Virginia" or "Mrs. Woolf," but these names referred to the person whom she was, not the author whom she will always be. An English writer, who had been on friendly terms with her when he was young, told me that she would have glared with contempt at anyone who referred to her as "Woolf" in violation of all her norms of courtesy and propriety.

THE INNER LIFE OF *MRS. DALLOWAY*

And more and more I come to loathe any dominion of one over another; any leadership, any imposition of the will.

—The Diary of Virginia Woolf, 19 March 1919

INTRODUCTION

Two Quests and a Sacrifice

M*rs. Dalloway* makes modest claims for itself. Its author, having first planned to call it *The Hours*, settled on a title consistent with its story about mostly unimportant people on an ordinary London day. She modeled the book in part on *Ulysses*, as James Joyce modeled his on the *Odyssey*, but her characters, unlike Joyce's, do not symbolize anything greater than themselves. "Genius it has," she wrote in her diary about *Ulysses*. But, she added, "It is brackish. It is pretentious." A "first rate writer," unlike Joyce, "respects writing too much to be tricky; startling; doing stunts." Joyce titled his book *Ulysses*, not *Mr. Bloom*.

The German critic Erich Auerbach seems to have been the first to recognize that Virginia Woolf, despite the apparent modesty of her subject matter, was not merely a major novelist but also a writer in the great epic tradition that began with Homer. Auerbach's magisterial and often thrilling survey, *Mimesis: The Representation of Reality in Western Literature* (1946), opens with the visible outer world of action portrayed in the *Odyssey* and closes—in an unmistakable tone of triumph—with the invisible world of the inner life portrayed in *To the Lighthouse* (1927). The epic writer whom Auerbach most loved was Dante, and

Auerbach saw in *To the Lighthouse* "a similarity to Dante's Comedy." Dante's poem found universal meanings in the events of a few days around Easter in the spring of 1300. Virginia Woolf's novel pointed toward universal meanings through the undramatic and (in Auerbach's phrase) "externally insignificant" events of two days: first, when a mother of eight gives a dinner party in her summer house in Scotland; then, ten years later, when one of her sons steers a sailboat expertly to an island, while, on the lawn outside the summer house, an amateur painter draws the line that gives order to her canvas. Auerbach's insight applies with equal force to *Mrs. Dalloway*.*

Dante's *Commedia* tells two quest stories. One quest is Dante's often arduous physical journey from Hell through Purgatory to Heaven. The other is the first quest's invisible psychological and spiritual counterpart, the passage of Dante's soul from despair through hope and onward to a beatific vision. In the modern world, where the events that seem to matter most in everyone's life are psychological and invisible—inward choices

---

* It is a striking fact of literary history that prominent male critics can convince themselves that Auerbach did *not* in fact end his book, as he emphatically did end it, with a chapter praising Virginia Woolf in a deeply personal way, a chapter in which he identified his own critical methods with her novelistic ones. Edward W. Said, in an introduction to a reissue of *Mimesis*, wrote that Auerbach compared himself to "modern novelists such as Joyce and Woolf"—a phrase that gives priority to Joyce, whom Auerbach mentions three times (one of them inside a parenthesis), over Virginia Woolf, who was the subject of Auerbach's whole chapter (*Mimesis: The Representation of Reality in Western Literature: Fiftieth-Anniversary Edition*, 2003, p. xxxi). Terry Eagleton, in a review of the same reissue, got the argument of Auerbach's chapter backward. "*Mimesis*," Eagleton wrote, "ends by rapping Virginia Woolf sternly over the knuckles." This eyebrow-lifting fantasy of critical corporal punishment seems to have sprung entirely from Eagleton's imagination ("Pork Chops and Pineapples," *London Review of Books*, 23 October 2023).

to act or not to act, to respond or not to respond—Virginia Woolf reduced the physical quests in her book to a few mostly trivial actions, like walking down a street or stepping onto a bus, and rendered the psychological quests with all the tension and excitement that earlier epics gave to public or physical ordeals and triumphs. In "Mr. Bennett and Mrs. Brown," her 1924 essay on the present and possible future of fiction, she described Mrs. Brown—an old woman glimpsed briefly on a train—as "very frail and very heroic": in other words, physically frail and inwardly heroic. Virginia Woolf ended *To the Lighthouse* at the moment when Lily Briscoe, who seems to herself and to everyone else an insignificant middle-aged spinster, makes a decisive inward choice to finish her painting, even though she cannot forget being told "Women can't paint," and even though her only visible act is to draw a line on her canvas and lay down her brush "in extreme fatigue."

Many characters in *Mrs. Dalloway*, like many in *Ulysses*, echo the far more powerful and effective characters in the *Odyssey*. Leopold Bloom and Peter Walsh are wanderers like Odysseus. Molly Bloom and Clarissa Dalloway are the women to whom Bloom and Peter return, as Odysseus returns to Penelope. Telemachus, sailing from island to island seeking news of his father, recurs in Stephen Dedalus and in Clarissa's daughter Elizabeth, two wanderers adrift in a city. The whole structure of *Ulysses* derives from its parallel between the ancient story and the modern one, and Virginia Woolf seems at first to have planned her novel—when she was still calling it *The Hours*—along the same set of parallel lines.

T. S. Eliot spoke with Virginia Woolf often about *Ulysses*, telling her it was a masterpiece. In 1923, around the time she was drafting *Mrs. Dalloway*, Eliot published a review essay, "*Ulysses*, Order, and Myth," in which he decreed that Joyce's method of "using the myth," of "manipulating a continuous parallel between contemporaneity and antiquity," was a method that later writers "must pursue after him." They had no choice in the matter. Joyce had not expressed a personal vision; he had made a discovery that other writers must use in the way that future scientists must use "the discoveries of an Einstein." History had made "the mythical method" inescapable, because, like any scientific discovery, it made sense of reality in ways that had not been recognized before: "It is simply a way of controlling,* of ordering, of giving a shape and a significance to the immense panorama of futility and anarchy which is contemporary history." Like many great scientific discoveries, it had been made by other investigators around the same time: "It is a method already adumbrated by Mr. Yeats." Eliot was also, elliptically, praising himself as a co-discoverer, having used "the mythical method" in *The Waste Land*, the poem published in book form by the Hogarth Press in 1923, with the type set by hand by Virginia Woolf while she was planning *Mrs. Dalloway*.

Virginia Woolf admired *The Waste Land*, but she was less convinced than Eliot either was or pretended to be that the force of history led inevitably to one kind of future, or that contemporary history offered only a spectacle of futility and anarchy. And at the deepest level of herself, she refused anyone's claim that she *must* do something, in the way that Eliot claimed that future writers "must" follow his method and Joyce's. *Mrs. Dalloway* is, among many other things, an extended protest against all authorities who say "must." As one character

---

* Eliot used *control* in the sense of its French and German cognates, "to keep account of something," a sense that survives in the English-language job title *controller*.

says of another: "'Must,' 'must,' why 'must'? What power had Bradshaw over him? 'What right has Bradshaw to say "must" to me?' he demanded."

The character who says this is the mad ex-soldier Septimus Warren Smith, speaking of the nerve doctor Sir William Bradshaw, whom the sane Clarissa, like the mad Septimus, recognizes as "obscurely evil" in the way that everyone is who says "must" about someone else, everyone who declares on behalf of health or justice what other people must do, what the future must do.*

This theme of the obscure evil of "must" seems to have played a role in Virginia Woolf's decision, while planning her book, to weave a second kind of story into the Odyssean narrative that she began with, a story with disturbing moral and psychological depths that *Ulysses* never achieves. She had begun writing her novel with the mythical method in mind, but she then complicated and transcended that method, portraying it explicitly as a psychologically fatal temptation: a temptation to passivity, to accept a world of "futility and anarchy" as something inevitable, something impossible to escape.

This counternarrative that she wove into the Odyssean story has its roots in the nineteenth century, not in the ancient world. It is one of many nineteenth- and twentieth-century stories of psychological doubles: two persons, one sober and self-controlled, the other violent and extravagant, whose lives are inextricable from each other even if they themselves, at first, know nothing

---

* But in *The Waves* (1931), Bernard, remembering the obligations of ordinary life, experiences a grateful converse of Septimus's thought: "Must, must, must. Must go, must sleep, must wake, must get up—sober, merciful word which we pretend to revile . . ."

of each other or of the connection between them. In a story about doubles, the two are so deeply entwined that the life or death of one depends in some real but mysterious way on the life or death of the other.

Victor Frankenstein and his creature are two such doubles. So are Golyadkin and his counterpart in Dostoyevsky's *The Double*,* Pip and Orlick in *Great Expectations*, and the title characters in *Dr. Jekyll and Mr. Hyde*. But the pair of doubles whom Virginia Woolf seems to have had in mind as her model when writing *Mrs. Dalloway* were Jane Eyre and the madwoman in the attic Bertha Mason, although no one explicitly identified them as doubles until many years after Virginia Woolf seems to have made use of them, probably without having consciously recognized them as doubles.†

She was aware of something troubling about the connection between Jane and Bertha, and she regarded *Jane Eyre* with something of the same kind of ambivalence that she felt about the genius of *Ulysses*. She wrote in *A Room of One's Own* about the moment when Jane suddenly hears Bertha laughing in her attic cell, although she thinks she hears Bertha's attendant Grace Poole and does not yet know that Bertha exists. The shift in perspective from Jane's meditations to Bertha's laugh:

---

* In a 1917 review, "More Dostoyevsky," Virginia Woolf acknowledged the "brilliancy and astonishing ingenuity" of *The Double*, but called it an "elaborate failure:" Dostoyevsky's "amazing machinery seems to spin fruitlessly in the air" (*Times Literary Supplement*, 22 February 1917).

† Adrienne Rich, in a 1973 essay ("Jane Eyre: The Temptations of a Motherless Woman," *Ms.*, October 1973; reprinted in her *On Lies, Secrets, and Silence*, 1979), first described Jane and Bertha as allies against patriarchy. Sandra M. Gilbert and Susan Gubar, in *The Madwoman in the Attic* (1979), expanded on Rich's insight by identifying them as doubles.

is an awkward break, I thought.... One might say, I continued, laying the book down beside *Pride and Prejudice*, that the woman who wrote those pages had more genius in her than Jane Austen; but ... one sees that she will never get her genius expressed whole and entire. Her books will be deformed and twisted. She will write in a rage where she should write calmly ...

Virginia Woolf wrote in an introduction to a 1928 American reprint of *Mrs. Dalloway* that "in the first version, Septimus, who later is intended to be her double, had no existence; and that Mrs. Dalloway was originally to kill herself, or perhaps merely to die at the end of the party."* Instead, Septimus dies on the afternoon of Clarissa's party, and Clarissa, confronted at the party with the fact of his death, finds through him, although she had never heard of him before, a psychological new life that until this moment had seemed to her impossible.

Septimus flings himself to his death from a second-story window in lower-middle-class London. Bertha Mason flings herself to her death from the roof of Thornfield Hall, and her death, by making her husband a widower, makes possible Jane Eyre's marriage to Mr. Rochester, whose domineering pride is humbled by the injuries he suffers in the fire set by Bertha, the fire that sent her to her death. At the time Virginia Woolf wrote her novel, no one seems to have noticed that everything Bertha

---

* What she calls "the first version" seems to have been the early stage when she was planning, and had begun writing, a sequence of stories about Clarissa and her circle. These plans changed sometime before 14 October 1922, when she wrote in her diary: "Mrs. Dalloway has branched into a book; and I adumbrate here a study of insanity and suicide; the world seen by the sane and the insane side by side—something like that. Septimus Smith—is that a good name?" There was no "first version" of the novel itself from which Septimus was absent.

does, although it terrifies Jane, invariably works to Jane's benefit. But Virginia Woolf's own genius let her understand the depths of genius she found in other writers, even those she half disapproved of, like Charlotte Brontë, like James Joyce.

Charlotte Brontë, by separating Bertha's death from Jane's marriage through a long interval of time and many pages of narration, conceals the logic through which the marriage issues from the death. Jane herself never sees the causal connection between the two events and remains entirely untroubled by it. As a result, Brontë's readers need not be troubled by the thought that one person's happiness may depend upon another's suffering. But Clarissa Dalloway, equipped with none of the causal links that Jane Eyre ignores, has the moral imagination to confront exactly that thought—"Somehow it was her disaster—her disgrace"—and that thought is one of the book's unsettling and insistent themes.* The doubles plot in *Mrs. Dalloway* derives from nineteenth-century sources, but Virginia Woolf has combined that plot with one that has ancient and religious roots: it is the story of one person's sacrifice for the sake of another person's redemption, the story at the heart of the Christian tradition that still resonated with a writer like Virginia Woolf, who mostly disdained that tradition and everything connected with it. Sir William Bradshaw, confronted in his consulting room by the mad Septimus, thinks contemptuously about a man who "comes into your room and says he is Christ (a common delusion)." Septimus imagines himself "the scapegoat, the eternal

---

* Characters named Richard and Clarissa Dalloway had minor roles in Virginia Woolf's first novel, *The Voyage Out* (1915); he was something of a cad, she was merely superficial. When Virginia Woolf began planning a novel about Clarissa Dalloway she seems to have intended to preserve their original characters. But the finished book makes Clarissa far more deep and Richard far more virtuous than they had been ten years before.

sufferer."* By combining a triumphant quest plot with a disturbing plot about sacrifice and redemption, Virginia Woolf created a work with breadth, depth, and concentrated density unlike anything else in modern literature.

Western literature of the past five hundred years has been the heir of different and conflicting inheritances. One is the classical tradition that uneasily combines the impulse toward abstract purity in Greek philosophy with the impulse toward bodily multiplicity in the pantheon of the Greek gods. In this tradition, character is fate; a person may be wise or reckless, but fate decides which; no one can choose a different life, no one can alter what fate has determined. The other inheritance is the monotheistic biblical tradition of moral commandments spoken by a single god presiding over a coherent universe, a god who commands you to change your life, but who grants you freedom to choose or refuse to obey his commandment. The first inheritance derives from Athens, the second from Jerusalem. At the heart of *Mrs. Dalloway* is an unresolved and unresolvable argument between these two inheritances—an argument that continues, always without any fantasy that it can ever be resolved, into Virginia Woolf's later novels.

Virginia Woolf had little patience with religion and belief, but she used religious language when she wanted to emphasize the deepest meanings of the things she cared about most. The inner life was one of those things, and in an essay on Montaigne, written while she was working on *Mrs. Dalloway*, she wrote about "this soul, or life within us." In *Mrs. Dalloway* the word "soul" occurs more than twenty times, almost always as a shorthand

---

* Virginia Woolf modeled Septimus partly on the sacrificial, epileptic Prince Myshkin in Dostoyevsky's *The Idiot* (I owe this insight to Ramathi Bandaranayake).

term for the life within us. Clarissa, for example, thinks of Sir William Bradshaw as capable of the indescribable outrage of "forcing your soul." The plot of sacrifice and redemption in *Mrs. Dalloway* has no overt religious meaning, but its deepest structure derives from the ancient Christian mythology that invisibly pervaded the atmosphere of Western European culture in which Virginia Woolf thought and wrote.*

And her version of that plot includes an uncanny and unexplainable connection between Septimus and Clarissa that makes it possible for her to understand his suffering and even imagine herself experiencing the sensations he endured in dying. Virginia Woolf wrote in her diary, while working on the book, about "my discovery; how I dig out beautiful caves behind my characters; . . . The idea is that the caves shall connect, and each comes to daylight at the present moment."

Those caves extend into depths still largely unexplored by readers and critics.

THE TWO QUESTS

Mrs. Dalloway tells the story of two heroic quests, each made partly through the outer world, partly through the world of "this soul, or life within us." Each quest requires a lonely, isolating descent into the land of the dead. Peter Walsh makes a quest

---

* The same plot is the structure that holds together the multiple incidents in *The Waste Land*, and was made intellectually respectable in twentieth-century culture partly by the influence of Sir James Frazer's *The Golden Bough*, which identified that plot as the source of all religions, Christian and non-Christian.

into the realm of inevitability and fate. Clarissa Dalloway makes a quest into the world of voluntary freedom.

Peter Walsh is Clarissa's disappointed suitor from thirty-three years earlier, now returning to England after three decades working as a colonial administrator in India, where he was married and divorced, and is now engaged to a woman almost thirty years younger than himself. He and his first wife seem to have had nothing in common beyond the "splendid time of it" that they enjoyed in bed. His new fiancée, with two small children by her first husband, seems to have little to offer him beyond the unlimited erotic satisfaction that she has joyfully promised him. In the years since Clarissa rejected him and married Richard Dalloway, Peter's personal life, in the past and now in his expected future, has been driven entirely by sex. But he has never stopped loving Clarissa, whom he has never even kissed. "One could not be in love twice," he says of his love for her. And now he has returned almost in secret: "nobody yet knew he was in London, except Clarissa," who in fact did not know, having forgotten the date when he would be there, "for his letters were awfully dull." In the background of this story is Odysseus returning after nineteen years to Ithaca and Penelope, after two involuntary sexual interludes with beautiful goddesses whom he could not bring himself to love. Odysseus was expert with spear and arrow; Peter annoys Clarissa with his pocketknife, "always opening and shutting a knife when he got excited."

Peter first appears in the book when he visits Clarissa's house in the morning of his first full day in England. He then wanders through London, at one point trailing at a discreet distance a young woman and fantasizing about offering her an ice. (She corresponds to the young princess Nausicaa in the *Odyssey*.)

Later he returns to his antiseptic hotel where he makes polite conversation with some fellow guests before leaving for Clarissa's party, in the way that Odysseus speaks courteously with his hosts on the island of Phaeacia before making his final landfall on Ithaca and his return to Penelope.

At one point in Odysseus's quest for home, he makes a detour to the land of the dead. There he meets his mother's spirit and sees the ghosts of many other women—so many, and so exclusively female, that the Phaeacian king to whose court he is telling the story interrupts to ask whether he had also met any ghosts of men. Peter himself makes a psychological journey to the realm of death during his wanderings around London, when he sits sleeping and dreaming on a park bench next to a "grey nurse" knitting beside him. "Down, down he sank into the plumes and feathers of sleep," and, as he snores, he dreams that he has ventured into a realm where persons have been replaced by myths that have inhuman grandeur—"something outside these miserable pigmies, these feeble, these ugly, these craven men and women." The nurse in her grey dress, transformed by his dream, "seemed like the champion of the rights of sleepers, like one of those spectral presences which rise in the twilight in woods made of sky and branches." And as the dream-Peter advances "down the path with his eyes on sky and branches he rapidly endows them with womanhood." He has entered a world of dream figures who have all the contradictory carnal and maternal attributes of conventional archetypes of women—archetypes being products of the imagination, not real persons of flesh and blood. These imaginary figures, conjured by his dream from trees and branches into womanhood, "dispense with a dark flutter of the leaves charity, comprehension, absolution, and then, flinging themselves suddenly aloft, confound the piety of their aspect with a wild carouse."

The feminine visions in Peter's dream tempt him to abandon the difficult reality of human beings for the simplicity of an archetype. The work of temptation is already half successful because Peter has dreamed himself into being the archetypal "solitary traveller," someone more generalizable, more impersonal, than Peter Walsh himself. That archetypal traveler exists in a fantasy world more comforting, less demanding than the real human world:

> Such are the visions which ceaselessly float up, pace beside, put their faces in front of, the actual thing; often overpowering the solitary traveller and taking away from him the sense of the earth, the wish to return, and giving him for substitute a general peace, as if . . . this fever of living were simplicity itself; and myriads of things merged in one thing; and this figure, made of sky and branches as it is, had risen from the troubled sea . . . to shower down from her magnificent hands compassion, comprehension, absolution.

Like the Sirens' song in the *Odyssey*, this vision—compassionate, comprehending, absolving—is a fatal trap. The peace it offers, the only "general peace" possible for human beings, is the peace of the dead, where human reality dissolves into emptiness: "So, he thinks, may I never go back to the lamplight; to the sitting-room; never finish my book; never knock out my pipe; never ring for Mrs. Turner to clear away; rather let me walk straight on to this great figure, who will, with a toss of her head, mount me on her streamers and let me blow to nothingness with the rest."

He has entered a world where "the rest," where everyone—not only himself—seeks nothingness: "So, as the solitary traveller advances down the village street . . . the evening seems ominous; the figures still; as if some august fate, known to them, awaited without fear, were about to sweep them into complete annihilation."

As the dream comes to its end, "Indoors among ordinary things, the cupboard, the table," Peter sees the landlady (Mrs. Turner, named earlier in the dream) clearing the table and hears her ask, "There is nothing more to-night, sir?" And the dream closes with the question: "But to whom does the solitary traveller make reply?" Mrs. Turner and the solitary traveler are two different kinds of beings in two different universes, one a person with a name, the other a nameless archetype, and they have no common language through which to speak with each other.

When Peter wakes, "with extreme suddenness," he exclaims to himself, "The death of the soul." He has no idea why he says this, but the phrase is Virginia Woolf's judgment on the whole idea of archetypal meanings and identities, an idea that murders "this soul, or life within us." A few hours after his hellish vision, near the end of the book, Peter finds the courage to ascend the steps to Clarissa's party. "The soul," he thinks, "must brave itself to endure." And his reward for his bravery here is the sudden revelatory vision that ends both the novel and his quest, when he asks himself, "What is this terror? what is this ecstasy? . . . What is it that fills me with extraordinary excitement," and realizes that "It is Clarissa. . . . For there she was."

Such is Peter's quest. Clarissa's quest follows a different path to terror, ecstasy, and excitement. Her outer quest begins in the one-sentence paragraph that opens the book: "Mrs. Dalloway said she would buy the flowers herself." It takes her then to Bond Street and back to her house in Westminster where she will remain, moving only between different floors and different rooms, until the end. This outer quest means almost nothing, although she walks past things that mean a great deal to other people. It is her inner, imaginative quest that, late in the book, transforms her.

Her quest, like Peter's, will take her to a realm of the dead, but to a very different kind of realm, one where the dead are real persons, not anonymous impersonal archetypes. The remaining chapters in this book will tell the story of that quest, which ends, in a simultaneous inward triumph, at the moment when Peter has his ecstatic vision of the person he thinks of as "Clarissa herself."

THE WORLD IN A BOOK

The great quest stories, from the *Odyssey* onward, tell stories that extend beyond the life and relationships of their heroes, beyond the world of the ordinary and the familiar. These stories open vistas onto worlds outside ordinary reality, worlds with customs, rites, and morals vastly different from that of their heroes and their authors. The pattern emerged fully formed in the *Odyssey*: the moral chaos of the Lestrygonians and the Cyclops, the monstrosity and danger of Scylla and Charybdis, the seductions of the Sirens—all these things recur across the centuries in different forms, each embodying some social or psychological temptation that the hero must escape.

In *Mrs. Dalloway* Peter Walsh's dream of annihilation—"the death of the soul"—is one such temptation. Others are Septimus Warren Smith's mad visions of "the whole world . . . clamouring: Kill yourself, kill yourself, for our sakes," and Peter's brief temptation to militarism when, seeing weak young boys marching to a war memorial, he feels pity for the dead general whom he had revered as a boy. But Peter, like any successful quest-hero, succeeds by refusing the temptations of pride, instead giving a charitable coin to an old woman begging for alms as she sings in the street.

 Novels tell stories that, typically, follow the King of Hearts's advice to Alice: "Begin at the beginning . . . and go on till you come to the end: then stop." They may recall events from a character's childhood, and may suggest what will happen after the final page, but they tend to evoke their characters' experience of time, focusing on their present moment, remembering their past, anticipating their future. Epics distinguish themselves from novels by reporting, in addition to the events that occur in the present time of their stories, events from a remote past and from a distant future. Aeneas hears a prophecy of future centuries; Dante learns of events dating back to the Creation.

 Mrs. Dalloway is both a novel—the story of a single day filled with recollections of events three decades earlier—and an epic that looks backward and forward to the remotest reaches of time. As Peter Walsh walks through London and passes the old singing woman to whom he gives his charity, the book suddenly looks back "through all ages—when the pavement was grass, when it was swamp, through the age of tusk and mammoth, through the age of silent sunrise," to the beginning of things. A summer thirty-three years ago is present in the lives of the characters in the ways that the remote past of Britain is present to the narrator: "as perhaps at midnight, when all boundaries are lost, the country reverts to its ancient shape, as the Romans saw it, lying cloudy, when they landed, and the hills had no names and rivers wound they knew not where . . ."

 The book also looks forward, toward a distant future in which antiquarians will probe the remains of the present day, "sifting the ruins of time, when London is a grass-grown path and all those hurrying along the pavement this Wednesday morning are but bones with a few wedding rings mixed up in their dust and the gold stoppings of innumerable decayed teeth." Like all great epics, *Mrs. Dalloway* raises questions about ultimate meaning, about what might ultimately matter—questions of value that no measurement, no enumeration of fact, can ever answer. The book quietly asks its reader: Which of the two survivals in the dust do you think matters more, the innumerable gold fillings left from teeth that have turned to dust, or the wedding rings, few as they are?

THE URBAN INVESTIGATOR

Virginia Woolf links Clarissa and Septimus across the barriers of class and geography by building two closely related literary genres into *Mrs. Dalloway*: the urban novel and the detective story. Both genres were invented in the nineteenth century, each in response to the rapid, sudden growth of metropolitan cities during the Industrial Revolution. Paris and London were the two cities that first expanded into a kind of social organization never known before: a city too large for any one person to comprehend, too complex and too fragmented for anyone to experience as a whole or as a home. Balzac and Dickens were the first novelists who felt the impulse to write a new kind of novel as a way of comprehending this new kind of city, and they each wrote stories that uncovered hidden connections between ways of life and social classes that occupied disparate parts of a city, places that to the eye of the casual observer seemed to have no connection at all—like the great mansion at Chesney Wold and the slum at Tom-All-Alone's in *Bleak House*.

The detective story seems to have emerged as a special form of the urban novel, one in which only the detective can intuit and expose the hidden connections that the urban novel explores.

The detective genre later escaped its urban origins and took up residence in villages, colleges, and remote islands, but it began in the slums and mansions of Paris and London. The earliest fictional detectives—Balzac's Vautrin, Poe's Dupin, Dickens's Inspector Bucket—solved mysteries that entangled other people, not the detective himself, who remained an objective observer, in effect an urban scientist. Clarissa Dalloway, when she intuits the cause of Septimus Warren Smith's otherwise unexplainable death (his local doctor sees it as cowardice), solves a mystery that implicates herself: "Somehow it was her disaster—her disgrace."

Mrs. Dalloway is dense with connections, some still waiting to be discovered, some more or less obvious. On the first page, Clarissa remembers how "she had burst open the French windows and plunged at Bourton into the open air." Much later, her double Septimus plunges from a window to his death. Then, as his wife Lucrezia drinks a sedative given her by a doctor, she imagines "that she was opening long windows, stepping out into some garden."

Both Clarissa and Septimus, one sane, one mad, withdraw into privacy, but Clarissa, after she confronts Septimus's death in the depths of her privacy, "felt somehow very like him—the young man who had killed himself." She is not entirely deceiving herself. She had experienced not only his death but also his fear. She too feels "the terror; the overwhelming incapacity." She too has "in the depths of her heart an awful fear."

Other connections seem more deeply hidden. Near the start of the book, Clarissa remembers the erotic visions that can sometimes occur when she is talking with a younger woman: "And whether it was pity, or their beauty, or that she was older, or some accident—like a faint scent, or a violin next door . . . , she did undoubtedly then feel what men felt. Only for a moment; but it was enough."

Many pages later, in much the same language, the book recalls that Miss Kilman—the woman in the book least like Clarissa and most opposed to her—found solace in religion: "and whether it was the music, or the voices (she herself when alone in the evening found comfort in a violin . . .), the hot and turbulent feelings which boiled and surged in her had been assuaged . . ."

Virginia Woolf maintains a double focus throughout the book, seeing the injustices of class—the differences, for example, that keep Clarissa alive and banish Septimus to death—while also seeing that different classes suffer from the same disorders of the will. The honored Sir William Bradshaw is a successful tyrant, the outcast Miss Kilman a failed one.

Miss Kilman is near the lowest end of the book's social scale. Near the highest is the upper-class toady Hugh Whitbread, with his "perfectly upholstered body" and "little job at Court." At Lady Bruton's lunch party midway through the book, her assistant Miss Brush observes that Richard Dalloway is genuinely glad to hear that Peter Walsh is back in London, while "Mr. Whitbread thought only of his chicken." A few paragraphs later, Hugh Whitbread keeps the rest of the party waiting while he finishes his lunch: "Hugh was very slow, Lady Bruton thought. He was getting fat, she noticed." That afternoon, Elizabeth Dalloway waits impatiently while Miss Kilman fingers the last two inches of a chocolate éclair ("I've not quite finished yet") before she finally swallows it.

The book's many echoes and parallels function as a kind of verbal connective tissue, holding together the disparate contents of the book through repetitions of sound and sense. Some of the echoes serve to emphasize the equality of souls—the equality of inner lives—that all of Virginia Woolf's books affirm even as they reaffirm the inequalities of class and status.* The book's most insistent echoes are its recurring sentences about the sound of Big Ben first repeating its melody, then striking the hour: "There! Out it boomed. First a warning, musical; then the hour, irrevocable. The leaden circles dissolved in the air."

Human beings perceive time in two contradictory ways: as a recurring series of cycles, and as a linear series of unique events. In cyclical time, events repeat themselves at more or less regular intervals, and nothing changes in any decisive way. The sun rises and sets; sleep is followed by waking which is followed by sleep; the heart beats; hunger alternates with repletion. In linear time, everything keeps changing once and for all. Aging is irreversible; one experience provokes or alters another one; a lost friend or a lost love can never be replaced; the hour is irrevocable.

Time in *Ulysses* is ultimately cyclical. Leopold Bloom, conscious of "the apathy of the stars," forgives everything that happens to him that he might have resented, and, as he sleeps, dissolves into archetypal multitudes: "Sinbad the Sailor and Tinbad the Tailor and Jinbad the Jailer," et al. Molly Bloom's closing soliloquy is shaped by the cycle of the seasons, and begins and ends with the same word, "yes." Human life in *Ulysses* is cyclical: a funeral occurs near the start of the book; a birth occurs near the end. No one confronts the possibility of his or her own unique irrevocable death. In cyclical time, individual choices don't matter, because everything is ultimately

---

* She wrote admiringly of Dostoyevsky: "It is all the same to him whether you are noble or simple, a tramp or a great lady.... The soul is not restrained by barriers. It overflows, it floods, it mingles with the souls of others" ("The Russian View," *Times Literary Supplement*, 19 December 1918; "The Russian Point of View," *The Common Reader: First Series* [1925]).

shaped by cycles that no one ever chooses, that no one could ever choose. The twentieth century was a great breeding ground for cyclical thought, as in Oswald Spengler's *The Decline of the West* (1918–1922), in which cultures are born, grow, and die like natural organisms shaped by recurring cycles of life and death, not by what Spengler saw as the ultimately futile choices made by individual persons.

Mrs. Dalloway sees everything differently. Life and death are not cyclical but determined by personal choice: Septimus chooses his own death when he commits self-murder. Civilizations rise and fall—the hills once had no name; London will someday be a grass-grown path—but wedding rings, each an enduring witness to someone's personal choice, persist in the dust. The leaden circles of cyclical time dissolve repeatedly in the air, and reconstitute themselves when Big Ben strikes again; but the hour, in linear time, is irrevocable. The plot of the book moves from one version of Clarissa Dalloway to a very different version of her. In the first sentence, "Mrs. Dalloway said she would buy the flowers herself." She has her husband's name and she chooses to act alone. In its final sentences, she has a name of her own and fills someone else with extraordinary excitement: "It is Clarissa, he said. For there she was."

W. H. Auden wrote of Virginia Woolf:

> What she felt and expressed with the most intense passion was a mystical, religious vision of life: "a consciousness of what I call 'reality': a thing I see before me; something abstract; but residing in the downs or sky; beside which nothing matters; in which I shall rest and continue to exist . . ."
>
> What is unique about her work is the combination of this mystical vision with the sharpest possible sense for the concrete, even in its humblest form.

In much of the twentieth-century literature that journalism labels "modernist," any mystical sense of things tends to dissolve the distinctions among those things. Generalizing archetypes and recurring historical cycles overwhelm any sense of individual persons—their individual value and their individual sufferings. Virginia Woolf, in the years after she wrote *Mrs. Dalloway*, wrote that she sometimes experienced a mystical sense of communion that joined every human being, sometimes thought "that in some vague way we are the same person, and not separate people." This thought was in the background of her novel *The Waves*. But at the time she was writing *Mrs. Dalloway* she focused on the intimacy that can join two unique individuals. In "Mr. Bennett and Mrs. Brown" she wrote about "the difficult business of intimacy" between a writer and a reader:

> The writer must get into touch with his* reader by putting before him something which he recognises, which therefore stimulates his imagination, and makes him willing to co-operate in the far more difficult business of intimacy. And it is of the highest importance that this common meeting-place should be reached easily, almost instinctively, in the dark, with one's eyes shut.

This was a remote form of "intimacy" between two persons who never meet, who may not even be alive at the same moment. After Septimus's death, an uncanny moment of remote intimacy joins him to Clarissa. The book combines her "mystical vision with the sharpest possible sense for the concrete," her sense of

---

* When writing about a generalized "writer" Virginia Woolf tended to use masculine pronouns as gender-neutral, even when she was clearly the writer she referred to.

the uniquely personal, the irrevocable, a sense of intimacy deep enough to triumph over death.

Comedy is the mode of literature in which, at the end, its characters escape death and join together in love. Tragedy is the mode in which its characters end up isolated and dead. *Mrs. Dalloway* is a comedy that, like all great comedies, is shaded by the possibility of death, by the death that Clarissa escapes and that other major and minor characters also escape. Peter, having escaped annihilation in his dream, thinks to himself that Clarissa's Aunt Helena, who had already been old when Clarissa rejected him, has long since died. Then, at Clarissa's party, he finds her sitting there, and the fact surprises him into a tautology: "For Miss Helena Parry was not dead: Miss Parry was alive." And he is still astonished a few pages later by this triumph of life: "Never had he had such a shock in his life! . . . He had been quite certain she was dead."

From *Mrs. Dalloway* onward, all of Virginia Woolf's later novels end in comedy's triumph over death—although only her last novel, *Between the Acts,* ends like *Mrs. Dalloway* in a triumph that includes love. At the end of *The Waves,* Bernard exclaims inwardly, "Against you I will fling myself, unvanquished and unyielding, O Death!" This is what *Mrs. Dalloway* says.

A PERSONAL NOTE

This book says almost nothing about Virginia Woolf's mental breakdowns in her earlier years. She made use of them in *Mrs. Dalloway* in more or less the same way she made use of her other experiences. For example, when she was young she had idealized a cousin's wife, Margaret Vaughn, almost twenty years older than herself, and remembered "washing my hands, and saying to myself 'At this moment she is actually under this roof.'" Clarissa remembers having idealized her contemporary Sally Seton, and saying aloud, "She is beneath this roof. . . . She is beneath this roof!" Virginia Woolf made use of the mad visions she had during her breakdowns by giving to Septimus Warren Smith some of their features, such as the moment when Septimus hears birds singing "in voices prolonged and piercing in Greek words, from trees in the meadow of life beyond a river where the dead walk, how there is no death."

More than once, when I was lecturing about Virginia Woolf in a university course, a young man asked, in tones resonating with pity, why I hadn't said more about her breakdowns. (The questioner was invariably a man pitying a woman's breakdowns; no one makes a point of pitying Hemingway's or T. S. Eliot's breakdowns.) The answer to the young man's question is the story that follows.

Many years ago I noticed a small growth on the back of my hand, which had been diagnosed as benign but which I wanted removed. When I went to the eminent plastic surgeon I had been referred to, I was appalled to see his hands shaking as we spoke. Then, while I worried over what might happen next, he took up his pencil and began writing notes in the most elegant italic script that I had ever seen. Later I learned that, among some of those who suffer from Parkinson's Disease, their hands become steady the moment they focus on them. The surgeon took up his scalpel and manipulated it so precisely that he left no scar.

The surgeon's hands did not shake when he was using his scalpel. Virginia Woolf's hands did not shake when she was writing.

1

MEDICINE

Among the hundreds of imagined characters in Virginia Woolf's novels, some are grasping and dishonest, some wounded and angry, but none is a villain: none pursues evil for its own sake. The one character who comes closest to villainy in all her novels is the distinguished physician, Sir William Bradshaw, a great nerve doctor—someone who a few years later would have been called a psychoanalyst. Sir William thinks of himself as a benevolent and civilizing force, acting for the good of his patients suffering psychological misery and for the good of society at large; had he existed in real life, he would have begun his career by taking the Hippocratic oath to do no harm. His consulting room is in Harley Street, the address favored by doctors at the height of their profession. Britain has honored him with power, prosperity, and a knighthood, and only a mostly silent few of the characters in *Mrs. Dalloway* see him differently. Clarissa thinks of him as "a great doctor yet to her obscurely evil," and Lucrezia Warren Smith, in her simpler but equally exact language, says he is "not a nice man."

Near the end of the book, when Sir William arrives at Clarissa's party, she needs a few moments to bring into clear focus what she had seen as obscurely evil about him. He is, she thinks, "without sex or lust, extremely polite to women, but capable of some indescribable outrage—forcing your soul, that was it." The verb "forcing" retains its earliest meaning, attested by the *Oxford English Dictionary*: to *force* is to *rape*, and Sir William's indescribable outrage—indescribable because obscene—is his invasive assault on the inner life of his patients.* Without sex or lust, Sir William's driving passion is, in Augustine's phrase, his *libido dominandi*, his lust to dominate. His honors and status are the products of a society that values his lust because it serves a larger social imperative to repress and control.

In four long paragraphs passing judgment on Sir William, Virginia Woolf's narrator gets to the heart of the matter. The narrator ends the third of those paragraphs by describing the relief felt by the "ten or fifteen guests of the professional classes," after experiencing an unaccountable "pressure on the top of the head" during dinner at Sir William's house, when they "breathed in the air of Harley street even with rapture; which relief, however, was denied to his patients."

Then the fourth of these paragraphs of authorial judgment describes the process by which, when a helpless patient is brought to his consulting room by despairing relatives, Sir William arranges to have him locked away in an asylum, freeing those relatives from their despair: "Naked, defenceless, the exhausted, the friendless received the impress of Sir William's will. He swooped; he devoured. He shut people up. It was this combination of decision and humanity that endeared Sir William so greatly to the relations of his victims."

---

* The soul that Sir William forces is—as tradition requires—feminine, because *anima* is a Latin feminine noun. Virginia Woolf always uses feminine pronouns for "our soul": as, for example, when Peter Walsh thinks about the soul who inhabits deep seas until "suddenly she shoots to the surface and sports on the wind-wrinkled waves."

"His patients" at the end of the preceding paragraph have become, at the end of this fourth paragraph, "his victims."

One of the many things wrong with Sir William's kind of medicine is that it relies wholly on the physician's power. He never thinks of medicine as something mutual between doctor and patient, a dialogue between the physician's skill and the patient's body and mind. He never imagines medicine as a process in which the patient responds to the physician's acts, or in which the physician chooses his acts according to the response he gets from his patient.

Sir William, the narrator reports in the four long paragraphs about his psyche, worships two goddesses, each an instrument of oppression: the goddess Proportion and the goddess Conversion. He requires his patients to accept his "sense of proportion," his sense that they should not take themselves overseriously or fuss over their personal tribulations. As in everyone's ordinary way of speaking, when Sir William speaks of a "sense of proportion" he means that you should see things his way, not yours. His way is impersonal and generalizing, indifferent to your suffering; proportion is a mathematical idea, not something that takes shape in anyone's unique psyche. The goddess Proportion seeks power to transform whole societies, not only individual persons: "Worshipping proportion, Sir William not only prospered himself but made England prosper, secluded her lunatics, forbade childbirth, penalised despair, made it impossible for the unfit to propagate their views until they, too, shared his sense of proportion . . ."

"Penalised despair" is Virginia Woolf's shorthand for any common mechanism of psychological oppression. And "forbade childbirth" is her protest against both public policy and personal constraint: her doctor forbade childbirth by telling her husband that she was psychologically too fragile for motherhood.

Sir William's nearest victim is his wife, Lady Bradshaw, whose soul he forced fifteen years ago:

> conversion, fastidious Goddess, loves blood better than brick, and feasts most subtly on the human will. For example, Lady Bradshaw. Fifteen years ago she had gone under. It was nothing you could put your finger on; there had been no scene, no snap; only the slow sinking, water-logged, of her will into his. Sweet was her smile, swift her submission . . .

Sir William's latest victim is Septimus Warren Smith, the young lower-middle-class veteran of the 1914–1918 War, whose officer was killed on the battlefield, and who later suffered a nervous breakdown as his repressed grief struggled to make itself felt. At noon on the day of the novel, Septimus's wife Lucrezia brings him to Harley Street for a consultation. Sir William, after exchanging a few words with them, makes arrangements for Septimus to be taken to a private asylum in the countryside. A few hours later, when Septimus imagines, wrongly, that someone has arrived at his flat to take him away on Sir William's authority, he kills himself by plunging from a window. A few hours later, Sir William is delayed on his way to Clarissa's party by a phone call reporting Septimus's death, and, when he arrives at the party, makes use of that death to make a point to Richard Dalloway about a Bill under discussion in Parliament.

No one expects love from a doctor, but the great physicians from Hippocrates to the present day taught that a doctor's care should take the form of sympathetic, unpossessive attention, something that has much in common with the attentions of love. W. H. R. Rivers, a great physician of Virginia Woolf's era, wrote the first clinical account of the disorder suffered by Septimus Warren Smith, which Rivers called "war-neurosis" and which almost everyone else called shell shock. Rivers reported that sufferers found relief by bringing to consciousness the horror that they had repressed. By bringing that unbearable horror into the light, they made it possible to transmute it into "the far more bearable emotion of grief."

With at least some of his patients, Rivers achieved this transformation through a talking cure: a slow, deliberate process that wove together the physician's "suggestion" and the patient's free, conscious choice of his response to that suggestion. Virginia Woolf never mentions Rivers, but he was famous in both literary and scientific circles, and specifically famous for his work on war-neurosis; she seems to have known about his way of thinking about disease even if she did not connect it with his name.

Sir William Osler, another prominent physician of Virginia Woolf's era, taught that a doctor should "care more particularly for the individual patient than for the special features of the disease." To care for the individual patient more than for the patient's symptoms was, Osler taught, the more effective means of bringing about a cure. It was also morally superior, and for Osler, as for Virginia Woolf, the more moral course of action generally proved to be the more practically effective one.

Sir William Bradshaw cares nothing for individual patients. When Septimus and Lucrezia arrive for their consultation he focuses only on Septimus's symptoms. He names the patient and his wife only in a parenthesis and reduces Septimus from a name to a member of a category, "the man":

> He could see the first moment they came into the room (the Warren Smiths they were called); he was certain directly he saw the man; it was a case of extreme gravity. It was a case of complete breakdown—complete physical and nervous breakdown, with every symptom in an advanced stage, he ascertained in

two or three minutes (writing answers to questions, murmured discreetly, on a pink card).

The physician, as Oliver Sacks wrote, "must always *listen* to the patient"; Sir William is "certain directly he saw the man" coming into the room, without hearing a single word. A few moments later Sir William observes another symptom: Septimus "was attaching meanings to words of a symbolical kind. A serious symptom, to be noted on the card." This is a moment that points toward one of Virginia Woolf's deepest themes. Unlike almost every other major writer at the time, she repeatedly expressed her emphatic distaste for "meanings . . . of a symbolical kind." In this novel and elsewhere, she wrote of symbolic meanings as distractions from reality that (in the words of Peter Walsh's dream) "pace beside, put their faces in front of, the actual thing." Most of her novels have moments when reality disappears behind a symbol, as in Bernard's exclamation in *The Waves*: "So the sincerity of the moment passed; so it became symbolical; and that I could not stand"; or moments when a symbol means nothing at all, as in *Between the Acts* (1941), where Colonel Mayhew's wife imagines herself staging a village pageant with "One window, looking east, brilliantly illuminated to symbolize—she could work that out when the time came." One of the last stories she wrote, "The Symbol," is about a woman's emotionally self-defeating and incoherent effort to convert real deaths into sentimental symbols.

Sir William sees rightly that Septimus is mad, but concludes wrongly that he should therefore be locked up. In the same way, Sir William sees rightly that Septimus's madness makes him attach meanings to words of a symbolical kind, but wrongly regards this as a symptom of a disease, not as Septimus's desperate attempt to evade the reality of his repressed grief. Peter

Walsh loves "Clarissa herself," not a symbolic image of her. Sir William Bradshaw values nothing for itself, and devalues everything as an object to be controlled.

By threatening to kill himself, Septimus has legally obliged Sir William to "certificate" him and have him sent by a magistrate to an asylum: "There was no alternative," Sir William explains to Lucrezia: "It was a question of law." Sir William's impulse to penalize and control arises from the same source as his focus on symptoms rather than patients. Both manifest not merely indifference to other people's uniqueness but an active hatred of it, a hatred that takes imposing symbolic forms: Sir William's goddesses, Proportion and Conversion, with their insatiable appetite for the human will.

Virginia Woolf wanted her novel to "give life and death, sanity and insanity," and show the social system "at work at its most intense." The one engine of the social system with the most focused power over life and death, sanity and insanity, is the medical profession. A physician has the unique power to give orders to a patient, orders of a kind that, outside of a court of law, no one else is empowered to give; and in Virginia Woolf's England a physician was obliged to direct a magistrate to give the orders that physicians could not give on their own.*

Of all Virginia Woolf's books, *Mrs. Dalloway* is the only one that attends throughout to the theory, practice, and legal power of medicine. In her other novels, people sicken and die, either from disease or their own hand, but those books have little or nothing to say about medicine. The incompetent South American doctor who does nothing for the dying Rachel Vinrace in *The Voyage Out* scarcely exists as a character. In *To the Lighthouse*

---

* This power had been codified in English law with the Lunacy Act of 1890.

Prue Ramsay dies in childbirth with no doctors visible anywhere. Only *Mrs. Dalloway* treats medicine as an insistent central theme. As Virginia Woolf wrote to a friend when the book was first published: "It was a subject that I have kept cooling in my mind until I felt I could touch it without bursting into flame all over. You can't think what a raging furnace it is still to me—madness and doctors and being forced."

Doctors are in the novel's foreground and background. The ones in the background are nameless: "a doctor" has told Clarissa to rest for an hour every afternoon; doctors seem to be the "they" in a phrase about her heart, "affected, they said, by influenza." The egregious snob Hugh Whitbread has come up to London with his wife Evelyn "to see doctors" about her unspecified female troubles. The doctors in the foreground have names and personalities: the Harley Street physician Sir William Bradshaw, the local general practitioner Dr. Holmes. The two have diametrically opposing views of health, medicine, and madness, but each has a wrong opinion about Septimus Warren Smith, and each sees him only as a set of symptoms manifested in the present moment, with no personal history worth thinking about.

THE BURDEN OF THE PAST

The action of *Mrs. Dalloway* takes place in a single day but, like all of Virginia Woolf's novels, the book tells many longer histories. Among its pervasive themes is the power of both the remembered past and the forgotten past to afflict the present. Septimus never recognizes that his breakdown originated five years earlier, when he was in the army and his officer was killed. One of the many things wrong with Sir William's idea of medicine is that, by caring only for the present-day symptoms of a disease, he ignores its etiology, the past events that provoked those symptoms into existence. Talking with Richard Dalloway at Clarissa's party about some proposed legislation—Richard is a member of Parliament—Sir William refers to "the deferred effects of shell shock." He knows the effects are deferred, but in his brief session with Septimus he takes no interest in the past causes of those deferred present effects.

In the novel, only Sir William calls Septimus's condition "shell shock," and Virginia Woolf seems to have been making a point by having him do so. In her letters and diary she never uses the term "shell shock" in her own voice, only when she quotes someone else using it. She seems to have had an unspoken conviction that to give a name to a psychological condition has the effect of treating as an object the person who suffers from it. That person becomes someone *with X*, not a person suffering from old wounds.*

Virginia Woolf felt strongly that human beings ought to be thought about in the language of verbs not nouns: what they *do* matters more than what they *are*. She wrote in a letter in 1933, "I meet somebody who says, 'you're this or that,' and I don't want to be anything when I'm writing." Those who see you as "this or that," she continued, include those, like Leonard Woolf's sister Bella, "who is kind and good, but as for seeing you, you might be a zebra or an elephant for all she sees of you." She was echoing the thoughts she had written eight or nine years earlier for Clarissa Dalloway: "She would not say of any one in the world now that they were this or were that . . . she would not say of Peter, she would not say of herself, I am this, I am that."

---

* A more recent term for Septimus's condition, a term referring to the deferred effects of trauma, and usually reduced to four familiar initials, tends to have the same depersonalizing effect.

One reason Clarissa can achieve her triumph of personhood and relationship at the end of the book is that she has thought this way—however trivial-sounding in its expression—from the beginning.*

W. H. R. Rivers wrote that war-neurosis was the product of repression. Soldiers, having witnessed horrifying events, repressed their memories of them by switching off any immediate emotional response. But this kind of repression succeeds only in daylight. At night the repressed terrors return, rushing through the sufferer's mind either as conscious thoughts or in dreams. The only cure that Rivers found effective was to encourage the soldier, calmly and carefully, to confront the emotions he was trying to repress. And this was best done through the slow process of the talking cure. "In such cases," Rivers wrote, "the greatest relief is afforded by the mere communication of these troubles to another." That theme recurs in many forms in *Mrs. Dalloway*, and seems to be the point of an apparent digression early in the book when the old, unhappy Mrs. Dempster, seeing an unhappy young woman in Regent's Park, "could not help wishing to whisper a word to Maisie Johnson; to feel on the creased pouch of her worn old face the kiss of pity."

Rivers learned this technique from Sigmund Freud, at a time when Freud was generally perceived as one among many psychological theorists, not yet as the unique leader of a triumphant psychoanalytic movement. Today, Freud and his theories, or the reputations of Freud and his theories, are commonly anathematized, but what Rivers learned from Freud was not Freudian

---

* Two characters in *The Waves*, published six years later, voice this same view. Louis says to himself, "these attempts to say, 'I am this, I am that'... are false," and almost immediately afterward, Neville rejects "these false sayings, 'I am this; I am that!'"

theories of sexuality. Instead it had to do with Freud's revolutionary transformation of psychological medicine from what it had mostly been, the study of generalizable symptoms, into what it became in psychoanalysis: the study of each patient's unique history, how each patient came to be that patient's unique present self.

W. H. Auden wrote of Freud, "if every one of his theories should turn out to be false, Freud would still tower up as the genius who perceived that psychological events are not natural events but historical." By "natural events" Auden meant events in cyclical time, events with physical and biological causes that are inescapable and impersonal and predictable by scientific laws. By "historical events" he meant events in linear time, unique, only partly predictable events provoked—not mechanically *caused*—by conscious or unconscious choices that depend on who is making them and when. Freud's method, Auden continued, implies "that every patient is a unique historical person and not a typical case." That phrase, "unique historical person," combines two ideas, each a corollary of the other, that are essential to *Mrs. Dalloway*: the idea that everyone is shaped by his or her own personal history, and the idea that everyone is unique.

Freud's work was published in English by the Hogarth Press, owned and managed by Leonard and Virginia Woolf. She was willing to publish Freud—starting in 1924—but, at the time she was writing *Mrs. Dalloway*, seems scarcely to have read him, and she remained doubtful about what she knew of his ideas until late in her life—when she suddenly started, as she said in her diary, "gulping up Freud." She saw that what psychoanalysts did for their patients—helping them to free themselves from the weight of their dead past—was precisely what she had achieved by writing *To the Lighthouse*: "I suppose that I did for myself what psycho-analysts do for their patients. I expressed some very long felt and deeply felt emotion. And in expressing it I explained it and then laid it to rest."

In *To the Lighthouse*, Lily Briscoe achieves her vision on the last page only after she has resolved her debilitating reliance on the dead Mrs. Ramsay; and two of the Ramsays' children free themselves from their constraining sense of their father as a tyrant. The same psychological issues occur in *Mrs. Dalloway*, where Septimus, through a medical failure, is destroyed by his past, while Clarissa, partly through her revulsion against that same medical failure, finds momentary release—"only for a moment; but it was enough."

The book records one day's events in London, but both Clarissa and Peter spend much of the day thinking back thirty-three years to a summer at Bourton, Clarissa's family home in the countryside. Clarissa* was eighteen; Peter was passionately in love with her; after weeks of mutual agony she rejected him, making the choice that shaped both their lives forever. Also that summer, as Clarissa was walking on the terrace at Bourton, her wild-child friend Sally Seton startled her into an intense moment of "revelation" by kissing her on the lips.

Clarissa's feelings for Sally faded afterward—today, "She could not even get an echo of her old emotion"—and she eluded Peter's passionate feelings by marrying Richard Dalloway, who is good-natured, generous, and even just, in some ways the moral center of the novel, but also shallow, conventional, and incapable of the depth and intensity that Clarissa felt with Peter Walsh and Sally Seton. Clarissa has long since repressed the unsettling excitements aroused by Peter and Sally, and she has lived with that repression all her adult life. The woman she most admires,

---

* Her father's name was Justin Parry, and her name would then have been Clarissa Parry, but that name never appears in the book. Peter Walsh thinks of her only as "Clarissa."

whom she wishes she could resemble, is Lady Bexborough, so self-controlled, so repressed, that she showed no emotion when, while opening a charity fair, she was handed a telegram telling her that her son had been killed in the war. Clarissa endorses precisely the thing that destroys Septimus Warren Smith: repression in the face of death.

Mrs. Dalloway, the novel published in 1925, evolved from a short story, "Mrs. Dalloway in Bond Street," which Virginia Woolf had published in 1923. In the short story Clarissa sees Lady Bexborough sitting upright in her carriage, and thinks that she, Clarissa, "would have given anything to be like that." Peter Walsh's phrase about Clarissa, when he remembers her early in the novel, "there she was, however; there she was," echoes a phrase in the short story where Clarissa thinks as she walks past Lady Bexborough "there she is." When Virginia Woolf reworked her short story as the first section of her novel, she retained Clarissa's sense of Lady Bexborough as the woman she most admired, but omitted the incident where Clarissa sees Lady Bexborough in person. Clarissa unknowingly suffers, unknowingly wounds herself, by wishing herself even more repressed than she already is; and by making Lady Bexborough invisible, the novel emphasizes, as the short story did not, that Clarissa's motive for suffering persists in her mind even without a reminder from the world outside.

THE INVISIBLE BURDEN

One of Septimus's two doctors, Dr. Holmes, thinks Septimus suffers from "nerve symptoms and nothing more." There is nothing wrong with Septimus, he says, that a game of cricket and a visit to the music hall can't fix. "Health," he says, "is largely a matter in our own control. Throw yourself into outside interests; take up some hobby." He himself owes his excellent health "to the fact that he could always switch off from his patients"—a phrase making clear that his connection with his patients is merely mechanical.

Septimus's other doctor, Sir William Bradshaw, takes the contrary view. To Sir William, Septimus has everything wrong with him—he is a "case of complete breakdown"—and nothing is in his own control, so the only way to treat him is to lock him away in an asylum with Sir William as attending physician.

Neither doctor asks nor cares what happened to Septimus in the past, which was this: As a boy, he left his lower-middle-class family in the provincial town of Stroud to come to London, imagining himself a poet. He found a job as a clerk in a firm of auctioneers and land agents, where his superiors admired his real and obvious abilities. Hoping (in the vocabulary of the time) to improve himself, he attended adult-education lectures on Shakespeare and fell dreamingly in love with the lecturer, Miss Isabel Pole. (Virginia Woolf, who had worked part-time giving the same sort of lectures, glances here at a lower-middle-class economy of adult education unlike the world where the Dalloways hire a private tutor for their daughter.) Septimus wrote love poems to Miss Pole, "which, ignoring the subject, she corrected in red ink." When war came, "Septimus was one of the first to volunteer. He went to France to save an England which consisted almost entirely of Shakespeare's plays and Miss Isabel Pole in a green dress walking in a square."

In the trenches he "developed manliness; he was promoted; he drew the attention, indeed the affection of his officer, Evans by name."* He and Evans grew attached to each other in the way that soldiers on the battlefield become brothers-in-arms.

---

* Virginia Woolf probably never thought about military ranks, thus her vague term "officer." A real Septimus would have enlisted as a private; his

The friendship was cheerfully unsymmetrical—"It was a case of two dogs playing on a hearth-rug; one ... snarling, snapping, giving a pinch, now and then, at the old dog's ear; the other lying somnolent"—and Evans, who, as Lucrezia observed, was "undemonstrative in the company of women," may have felt a stronger attachment. Then: "When Evans was killed, just before the Armistice, in Italy, Septimus, far from showing any emotion or recognising that here was the end of a friendship, congratulated himself upon feeling very little and very reasonably. The War had taught him."

Only later, after the Armistice, billeted in an inn in Milan, Septimus discovered, to his terror, that it was not only Evans about whom he had no feelings: he had no feelings about anything at all. He experienced "sudden thunder-claps of fear. He could not feel." He made a desperate effort to suppress his fear by proposing marriage to the innkeeper's daughter Lucrezia: "he became engaged one evening when the panic was on him—that he could not feel."

Back in England, married to Lucrezia, he begins to disintegrate. He sees a dog transforming into a man; he sees Evans still alive; birds speak to him in Greek. He refuses sex. When his wife puts her arms around him, her cheek next to his, he thinks: "Love between man and woman was repulsive to Shakespeare. The business of copulation was filth to him before the end. But, Rezia said, she must have children. They had been married five years."

And he has lost the sense that Lucrezia or anyone else is really there. He imagines that "human nature" has condemned him to death for the great crime of being unable to feel.

---

promotion would have made him a corporal, and his officer, Evans, would have been his sergeant.

Lucrezia takes her husband to Sir William Bradshaw when she realizes that Dr. Holmes can do nothing for him. Sir William does worse than nothing by arranging to lock him away. Sir William specializes in, among other things, the kind of lie achieved by euphemism. When Lucrezia asks if Septimus is mad, "Sir William said he never spoke of 'madness;' he called it not having a sense of proportion," not being willing to suppress one's own perception of reality in favor of one endorsed by the world.

(Twenty-first-century readers may be tempted to congratulate themselves for living in an age that knows far more about the mind than Sir William imagined. This is not quite the case. While many modern successors to the nerve doctors of 1925 still focus, as W. H. R. Rivers did, on a patient's personal history, others, empowered by technology, tend to focus their attention on symptoms, somewhat as Sir William did—although the symptoms that they focus on are neurons flashing in a brain scan. These symptoms are invisible to the unaided eye, but are symptoms all the same. Sir William's modern counterpart is infinitely more sophisticated than he was, but no less indifferent to what might have happened years ago in the patient's life, what might have served to provoke the symptoms that manifest themselves in the present moment of a brain scan.)

The talking cure requires a relation of trust and care between two persons, unlike cures that might be induced through drugs, surgery, diet, rest, exercise, or impersonal relations. The "difficult business of intimacy" between doctor and patient, the form of intimacy that Virginia Woolf hoped to achieve between writer and reader, is what makes the talking cure possible.

Sir William prescribes isolation, not intimacy. "We have been arranging that you should go into a home," he says. "One of *my* homes, Mr. Warren Smith, where we will teach you to rest." *We* will teach *you*; the plural collective authority of *we* is what will command the singular individual person. And the "home" ("one of *my* homes") that Sir William has chosen for him is emphatically not a home in any real sense. Isolation is essential there. Lucrezia wants to be near her husband, and asks if he will be sent away from her. "Unfortunately, yes," Sir William answers: "the people we care for most are not good for us when we are ill." W. H. R. Rivers's talking cure was a means by which the patient arrived at self-knowledge. Sir William instead tells Septimus, "Try to think as little about yourself as possible."

For Dr. Holmes, "health is largely a matter in our own control." Sir William makes health a matter of other people's control of the sick person. And he traces mental disease partly to genetic factors that we can never control because we inherit them biologically: "unsocial impulses," he assumes, are "bred more than anything by the lack of good blood." Hence his impulse to forbid childbirth.

THE RETREAT FROM MOSCOW

As Virginia Woolf wrote in her 1928 introduction to the novel, she intended Septimus to be Clarissa's double. Part of the genius of the book is the way in which both Septimus and Clarissa suffer illness and isolation, and both suffer through repression, but—and here Virginia Woolf's sense of justice and injustice is at its sharpest—Clarissa survives because she, daughter of an old landed family, married to a Member of Parliament, is safely cushioned by her upper-class social world, while Septimus dies because he is a lower-middle-class outsider without family, status, money, or friends.

Clarissa, unlike Septimus, accepts the isolation that her husband offers her in service to her health. Although the book never spells it out—because Clarissa never consciously admits it to herself—she has never fully recovered from the influenza she suffered during the epidemic of 1918–1919, when vast numbers of people died, although the world, like Clarissa, seemed mostly to forget it afterward. The worst phase of the epidemic occurred late in 1918, so Clarissa may have caught the disease around the same time, after the Armistice in November 1918, when Septimus began to experience the war-neurosis.

Clarissa sleeps alone, in a separate bedroom at the top of the stairs, because her husband doesn't want to disturb her when he comes home late from Parliament: "For the House sat so long that Richard insisted, after her illness, that she must sleep undisturbed." In fact, "she slept badly," even when undisturbed by Richard. "She had read late at night of the retreat from Moscow. . . . And really she preferred to read of the retreat from Moscow. He knew it."

At the heart of Virginia Woolf's moral vision is her clear sense that it is not merely other people who isolate those in need—not merely the obscurely evil like Sir William Bradshaw or those of whom we can be comfortably certain that they are not at all like us. In Virginia Woolf's world, as in reality, everyone excludes someone in need, often for motives that seem both generous and sympathetic. Richard Dalloway, uxorious and considerate, encourages Clarissa to sleep alone, as she prefers, and does his best to keep silent on the staircase when he comes home at night. His motives are medicinal: he wants to protect her health. He has none of Sir William Bradshaw's lust for dominion, none of Dr. Holmes's indifference. But the effect of his actions, like theirs, is to isolate, not connect.

And Clarissa herself is complicit in Richard's isolating acts. She has been reading the memoir by the French general Baron Marbot of Napoleon's disastrous retreat from the city that froze out the invader—as her own inner coldness has induced her husband's retreat from herself. That retreat was his considerate, selfless response after she had, in her own eyes, "failed him" erotically, again and again. She recognizes the cold spirit inside herself; it was "through some contraction of this cold spirit, she had failed him." Septimus in his madness rejects sex, rejects his wife's desires. Clarissa merely feels detached from sex—although she has intense erotic feelings that she keeps hidden from everyone—and she prefers, with her husband's blessing, to sleep alone.*

Septimus has gradually withdrawn into insane isolation after the sudden death of someone he loved as a brother-in-arms. In one of the book's many well-hidden doublings, Clarissa too seems to have withdrawn into isolation after the sudden death of a loved sibling. It happened when she was young, and was caused by "that querulous, weak-kneed old man," as Peter remembers him, "Clarissa's father, Justin Parry." Peter remembers Clarissa talking about it long ago, in a phase of her life when she was bitter about fate: "That phase came directly after Sylvia's death—that horrible affair. To see your own sister killed by a falling tree (all Justin Parry's fault—all his carelessness) before your very eyes, a girl too on the verge of life, the most gifted of them, Clarissa always said, was enough to turn one bitter." (In an understated detail, Sylvia's name derives from the sylvan woods that killed her.)†

---

* She refuses the kind of intimacy that Virginia Woolf mentions in her diary (28 February 1927): "Last night I crept into L.'s bed to make up a sham quarrel about paying our fares to Rodmell." Or, as Bernard says in *The Waves*, "Going up to bed we settled our quarrel on the stairs."

† Sylvia's name occurs only twice in the book: here, and in the opening pages where, walking through London, Clarissa "remembered Sylvia, Fred, Sally Seton—such hosts of people." Fred is not mentioned again. Clarissa has a

Clarissa responded to her sister's death by suppressing her inner life, by choosing to live with dignified decency according to the values of the outer life: she kept a stiff upper lip. Peter reconstructs her thinking:

> possibly she said to herself, As we are a doomed race, chained to a sinking ship . . . as the whole thing is a bad joke, let us, at any rate, do our part; mitigate the sufferings of our fellow-prisoners . . . decorate the dungeon with flowers and air-cushions; be as decent as we possibly can. Those ruffians, the Gods, shan't have it all their own way—her notion being that the Gods, who never lost a chance of hurting, thwarting and spoiling human lives, were seriously put out if, all the same, you behaved like a lady.

Clarissa "behaved like a lady," as Septimus "congratulated himself upon feeling very little and very reasonably." Both accept the values of a culture that has little patience with suffering. Clarissa admires Lady Bexborough's stoicism. When the aristocratic Lady Bruton asks Clarissa, "And how are you," Clarissa lies that she is "perfectly well," because she knows that "Lady Bruton detested illness in the wives of politicians." Evelyn Whitbread, coming to London to see doctors, is pitiable in a vague way that refuses sympathy, having an illness which, her husband Hugh Whitbread knows, Clarissa "would quite understand without requiring him to specify." For upper-class women as for lower-middle-class veterans, illnesses must not be named. Clarissa, thinking early in the day about what Peter Walsh might say about her when they meet, represses the word "influenza," using instead the vague anodyne word "illness": "Since her illness she had

---

brother, Herbert, who, she says later, now lives at Bourton; that is all we know about him.

turned almost white." And later, when Clarissa remembers that "Richard insisted, after her illness, that she must sleep undisturbed," Richard is as tactfully vague as she is. In a culture that worships strength at best and stoicism at worst, illness is unnamable and unforgivable.

Everyone in the book tries to avoid talking about illness, either to themselves or to anyone else. The men who think about it at all tend to think of it as unmanly, like Dr. Holmes urging Septimus to throw himself into some vigorous sport. Women tend either to think it shameful, like Lady Bruton, or, like Clarissa, with a trace of contempt for other women's "usual interminable talk of women's ailments." The words "robust" and "robustness" recur throughout the book,* pointing to a quality that everyone in the world of this novel thinks of as admirable, a quality that neither Septimus nor Clarissa enjoys. The aptly named Lady Bruton, however, has "her ramrod bearing, her robustness of demeanour," and even Miss Kilman has her "robustness, and power." To be weak or ill is not only to be denied sympathy but also to refuse sympathy to others. Septimus Warren Smith drops his wife's hand and rejoices in his mad sense that his marriage has ended. When Richard Dalloway sympathetically spares Clarissa from disturbance to her nighttime rest, his sympathy takes the form of withdrawal, so that she sleeps alone and prefers it.

As Septimus goes mad, his repressed terrors emerge in their distorted forms. As he drifts toward sleep, on the last night of his life, the sounds of other people recede and he interprets the silence as abandonment. "They had lost him! He started up in terror." Clarissa, many years after her sister's death, still lives in a state of apprehension. At a florist's shop early in the morning,

---

* David Bradshaw first noted this in his Oxford World's Classics edition, which also notes many other recurring, lightly hidden themes.

she hears "oh! a pistol shot in the street outside!"—or so, in her alarm, she imagines it. The florist, who does not suffer Clarissa's fears, recognizes the sound of an engine backfiring, and says merely, "Dear, those motor cars." The sound "made Mrs. Dalloway jump and Miss Pym go to the window and apologise."*

As Clarissa's day begins, she is conscious that "She had a perpetual sense . . . of being out, out, far out to sea and alone; she always had the feeling that it was very, very dangerous to live even one day." At midnight, in the little room, she thinks: "Then (she had felt it only this morning) there was the terror; the overwhelming incapacity . . . ; there was in the depths of her heart an awful fear." Both Septimus and Clarissa respond to their terror with the one action that can only make it worse: they insist on refusing the only possible escape from the isolation that terrifies them.

COMMUNICATION IS HEALTH

For Clarissa, as for Septimus, the only hope of healing is to communicate with others, either in some intimate connection that can break their joint isolation, or in something like W. H. R. Rivers's talking cure. Both Clarissa and Septimus know this, although Septimus knows it only through the distorting lens of madness. In the essay on Montaigne that Virginia Woolf wrote while working on *Mrs. Dalloway*, she paraphrased him in a manner that suggests that she wanted to say in her own voice exactly

---

* Clarissa's fear was less visible in the 1923 story "Mrs. Dalloway in Bond Street," where the explosion in the street makes the shopwomen cower behind the counters while it merely prompts Clarissa, still sitting very upright, to remember another customer's name: "'Miss Anstruther!' she exclaimed."

what Montaigne had said in his—especially about "health and sanity." One such paraphrase was this: "Communication is health; communication is truth; communication is happiness. To share is our duty; to go down boldly and bring to light those hidden thoughts which are the most diseased; to conceal nothing; to pretend nothing; if we are ignorant to say so; if we love our friends to let them know it."

Septimus, unsettlingly, expresses from the depths of his madness many of these sane, clarifying thoughts. He imagines himself in Greece not London, and thinks Evans is alive: "So there was a man outside; Evans presumably; and the roses, which Rezia said were half dead, had been picked by him in the fields of Greece. Communication is health; communication is happiness. Communication, he muttered."

Earlier in the novel, his mind wandering, he thinks in some ways—not in others—that are characteristic of the rest of the book and its author:

> Men must not cut down trees. There is a God. (He noted such revelations on the backs of envelopes.) Change the world. No one kills from hatred. Make it known (he wrote it down). He waited. He listened. A sparrow perched on the railing opposite chirped Septimus, Septimus, four or five times over and went on, drawing its notes out, to sing freshly and piercingly in Greek words how there is no crime and, joined by another sparrow, they sang in voices prolonged and piercing in Greek words, from trees in the meadow of life beyond a river where the dead walk, how there is no death.

"Men must not cut down trees." This seems a distorted response to the rotting tree that, because a man failed to cut it down, killed Clarissa's sister when it fell. The birds that sing in Greek are the birds that Virginia Woolf recalled hearing when she lay in bed in 1904 "thinking that the birds were singing Greek choruses and that King Edward was using the foulest possible language . . ." (this from a memoir, "Old Bloomsbury," written in 1922, around the time she began *Mrs. Dalloway*). As for there being "no death," this too corresponds to Clarissa's "transcendental theory," as Peter Walsh remembers it, a theory:

> which, with her horror of death, allowed her to believe, or say that she believed (for all her scepticism), that since our apparitions, the part of us which appears, are so momentary compared with the other, the unseen part of us, which spreads wide, the unseen might survive, be recovered somehow attached to this person or that, or even haunting certain places, after death. Perhaps—perhaps.

Septimus's doctors never think of offering him the kind of communication that might lead him back to health, and he refuses the intimacy that Lucrezia offers him. Clarissa has spent most of her life closed off from intimacy, but unlike Septimus she has some insight into what she has refused:

> She could see what she lacked. It was not beauty; it was not mind. It was something central which permeated; something warm which broke up surfaces and rippled the cold contact of man and woman, or of women together. For *that* she could dimly perceive. She resented it, had a scruple picked up Heaven knows where, or, as she felt, sent by Nature (who is invariably wise) . . .

Clarissa's sense that her coldness was sent by Nature is morally and intellectually the same neurobiological fallacy sometimes found in medical thinking a century later: the fallacy that uses something impersonal, chemical, biological, natural, to explain unhappiness, not something that you or someone else did in the past, something like that moment long ago when Sylvia was killed by a falling tree, killed by her own father's patriarchal incompetence, the moment that thrust Clarissa into a life of mourning, like Electra mourning her sister Iphigenia sacrificed by their father Agamemnon.

By weaving the tangled strands of Septimus's thoughts together with the strands of Virginia Woolf's own thoughts—her sane thoughts in the present, her mad thoughts in the past—she achieved something complex and profound. She was never tempted by the wishful idea, recurring throughout history, that the mad have wisdom inaccessible to the sane; she hated her episodes of madness, and, fifteen years later when she killed herself, she seems to have done so as an act of defiance, a refusal to let herself be trapped in another episode of madness. But she also understood that the thoughts provoked by madness can be distorted images of truths that are less directly accessible to the sane. (Auden wrote in the 1930s that psychology, by excluding social reality, "ignores the fact that the neurotic has a real grievance": one's response to an event may be neurotic or insane, yet the event is all too real.)

One of Virginia Woolf's motives in writing *Mrs. Dalloway* seems to have been a wish to kill off the mad part of herself in the person of Septimus Warren Smith, so that the sane part of herself, in the person of Clarissa Dalloway, might emerge from its unhappiness and choose to emerge from isolation—like Clarissa in the last moments of the book, when she comes back from the little room, having chosen to "assemble," to "find Sally and Peter," two convenient names for all the loves that Clarissa has evaded until now.

As the only way out of Septimus's isolation is through the talking cure that no one thinks of offering him, so, for Clarissa, as for her author, the only way out of isolation is through communication. Through most of the book, Clarissa has refused communication. The one intimate, communicating moment that she experiences on this day seems to her to occur almost by accident, but it results directly from her revulsion against Sir William Bradshaw and his style of medicine. When Lady Bradshaw tells her that a young man has killed himself, Clarissa, angry at the intrusion of death, withdraws into the solitude of the little room. There she makes an uncanny connection with the dead Septimus whom she has never met and whose name she does not know, but whose death she experiences in imaginative sympathy, and perceives as an act of communication with her living self.

How this happens, and its transforming effect on her, is one of the subjects of my third chapter. Meanwhile, my second chapter takes up the theme of empire that the book glances toward at the moment when Clarissa steps into the little room and finds it empty. What she sees is a specific and sharply focused kind of emptiness: two unoccupied chairs that silently say a great deal about status and power, about politics and gender: "The chairs still kept the impress of the Prime Minister and Lady Bruton, she turned deferentially, he sitting four-square, authoritatively. They had been talking about India."

2

EMPIRE

"They had been talking about India." Clarissa has walked into the little room where, a few minutes earlier, the Prime Minister and Lady Bruton had found a private place to talk: "Old Lady Bruton, and she looked very fine too, very stalwart in her lace, swam up, and they withdrew into a little room which at once became spied upon, guarded, and a sort of stir and rustle rippled through every one openly: the Prime Minister!"

Lady Millicent Bruton is the woolly-minded, self-satisfied, and formidably aristocratic political hostess driven by a dim idea of using the British Empire and Commonwealth as a means of managing population. "Empire," the narrator reports, is Lady Bruton's goddess, as Proportion and Conversion are Sir William Bradshaw's goddesses, and she "had acquired from her association with that armoured goddess her ramrod bearing, her robustness of demeanour . . ."

When she and the Prime Minister return from the little room, the toady Hugh Whitbread is waiting for them: "Look at him now, on tiptoe, dancing forward, bowing and scraping, as the Prime Minister and Lady Bruton emerged, intimating for all the world to see that he was privileged to say something, something private, to Lady Bruton as she passed."

The whole episode brings the highest level of politics into the private sanctum that the little room briefly becomes when the Prime Minister and Lady Bruton enter into it for their secret consultation.

After the Prime Minister leaves the party, and Sir William and Lady Bradshaw arrive, with Lady Bradshaw using a young man's suicide as their excuse for lateness, Clarissa, unsettled by the presence of death at her party, walks into the little room, with no sense of what to expect.

At this point the narrator makes some observations that are more telling than they may seem:

> Perhaps there was somebody there. But there was nobody. The chairs still kept the impress of the Prime Minister and Lady Bruton, she turned deferentially, he sitting four-square, authoritatively. They had been talking about India. There was nobody. The party's splendour fell to the floor, so strange it was to come in alone in her finery.

This, with all its deep and serious meanings, is a wonderfully comic moment. The signs of Lady Bruton's deference and the Prime Minister's authority are the imprints of their buttocks on empty chairs, "she turned deferentially, he sitting four-square, authoritatively." Their postures are signs of sexual and political hierarchy, and what they were talking about, India, is a matter of imperial hierarchy. It is the narrator, not Clarissa, who knows what they were talking about, and who connects it to their postures.

But no one is actually there, only the impressions left on two chairs. And the book says many things when it says, twice in the same paragraph, "there was nobody." No persons are present, but the signs of power and power relations are very much present, because—and this is one of Virginia Woolf's great themes—power, in order to exert its dominion, does not require the actual or visible presence of powerful persons. In fact, it does not require their existence at all, and their physical presence diminishes its authority. The Prime Minister himself, as the novel reports on his arrival at the party, has no personal power at all: "One couldn't laugh at him. He looked so ordinary. You might have stood him behind a counter and bought biscuits—poor chap, all rigged up in gold lace."

This figure, in effect an empty suit, is only one of the many empty or invisible embodiments of power worshiped by almost everyone in the world of this book. My first chapter focused on the kinds of personal power that a doctor, for example, can wield over an individual patient. This chapter focuses on the kinds of impersonal power that can seem to be wielded by no one at all—by power in some abstract form—over impersonal collectives like a class or a nation, or over that chimerical abstraction, the public.

Earlier in the day, Lady Bruton had invited Richard Dalloway and Hugh Whitbread to lunch in the hope of furthering her idea of sending unemployed and economically superfluous young men to the colonies where they could find work. Lady Bruton is "a strong martial woman, well nourished, well descended, of direct impulses, downright feelings, and little introspective power." The imperial idea of exporting young people has filled her psyche to the point where "Emigration had become, in short, largely Lady Bruton."

Lady Bruton has power in the empire, but no power over language.* She has brought Hugh and Richard to lunch so that

---

* W. H. Auden, "August 1968": "About a subjugated plain, / Among its desperate and slain, / The Ogre stalks with hands on hips / While drivel gushes from his lips."

Hugh can write the letter she wants to see printed in the *Times* about her scheme of emigration: "she had to write. And one letter to the *Times* . . . cost her more than to organise an expedition to South Africa (which she had done during the war)." Hugh Whitbread writes her pompous letter for her, a letter that Richard silently "thought all stuffing and bunkum."

Lady Bruton is personally absurd, but her power, now as in the war, is real. The novel makes the subtle suggestion that she is an insider of a surveillance society through which the actions of ordinary citizens are monitored by the state. Peter Walsh is convinced that no one but Clarissa knows he is in London. But Lady Bruton knows: "'D'you know who's in town?' said Lady Bruton suddenly bethinking her. 'Our old friend, Peter Walsh.'" And when Hugh Whitbread asks for Peter's address, "grey-haired Perkins, who had been with Lady Bruton these thirty years and now wrote down the address; handed it to Mr. Whitbread." How does she know? The prosaic explanation is that lists of arriving steamship passengers are official documents, routinely filed in a government office, and someone in Whitehall has told Lady Bruton; but the book gives no explanation, suggesting only that Lady Bruton is near to the center of a network of knowledge that knows everything about citizens who are unaware that it exists.*

---

* The novel never says it explicitly, but Peter has presumably alerted his lawyers and solicitors, Messrs. Hooper and Grateley of Lincoln's Inn, that, as he tells Clarissa, he expects them to arrange his divorce. In *Night and Day* (1919) the firm had been named both Grateley and Hooper and Hoper [*sic*] and Grateley. In the real world it was Roper and Whateley, who employed one of Virginia Woolf's brothers-in-law.

FICTION AND FREEDOM

Virginia Woolf, like Clarissa, would not say of herself that she was *this* or was *that*, and it is impossible to say that what *Mrs. Dalloway* is about is *this* or is *that*. But it may be possible to say, tentatively, what all literature is about. The ultimate subject of literature, as of all the arts, may be personal freedom, beginning with an artist's personal freedom to make this particular work rather than any of an unlimited set of alternatives, and continuing with the content of the work of art itself.

When I say something like this aloud, someone is likely to protest that this thought is too Western, too Eurocentric, too modern, or too bourgeois to take seriously. Perhaps the doubtful can be reassured by what seems to be the fact that every culture in the world tells stories in which a young woman does not want to marry the man whom her father has chosen for her. She wants either to marry no one at all or to marry the person she has chosen for herself. These stories, in their multitudes of form, often end in tragedy, but whenever such a story is told, it affirms that a young woman's personal freedom matters. That young woman is typically the least powerful person in her society, the one person most subject to traditional authority and rules. But if the freedom of the least powerful person matters, then, in that social world, and everywhere else, everyone's freedom matters.

One of the things such stories are about—and this will be a theme of my third chapter—is everyone's freedom, or what ought to be everyone's freedom, to choose the life of one's own body as well as the life of one's own mind. In the mind of the young woman, in every version of this story, her body is not her father's property, nor the property of her family, clan, class, culture, or nation. Its future is, or ought to be, hers to choose. To say that this kind of story, this kind of freedom, is narrowly Eurocentric or bourgeois, or the effect of unearned privilege, seems to me narrowly Eurocentric and bourgeois, as well as pernicious and false.

One of the most disturbing things about *Mrs. Dalloway* is the way in which everyone in it, now or in the past, has voluntarily sacrificed freedom in order to serve purposes that are not worth serving, purposes that do no good to anyone. Everyone yields to some idea; obeys rules that no one imposes; serves causes that no one asks them to serve. The most obvious instance of this theme is the imperial theme of British majesty and the British Empire. Many other and less obvious instances also pervade the book.

During the novel's single day in London in June 1923, its characters keep thinking about things that happened in the distant past and in distant places. ("It took me a year's groping," Virginia Woolf wrote in her dairy in 1923, "to discover what I call my tunnelling process, by which I tell the past in installments, as I have need of it.") Many of the things they think about are variations on the theme of empire and on other varieties of cultural and national power. A motif that recurs through all this is the contrast between, on the one hand, the deferential awe that people feel in the presence of power and, on the other hand, the emptiness, even the triviality, of the persons who wield power or embody it, and of the objects that symbolize it.

The Prime Minister, in his futile attempt "to look somebody" at Clarissa's party, is amusing to watch if you are Clarissa, with her upper-class ancestry and status. But something more subtle and dangerous, along much the same lines, happens to Clarissa and everyone else earlier the same day, when Clarissa is in a flower shop and hears an engine backfiring outside:

The violent explosion which made Mrs. Dalloway jump and Miss Pym go to the window and apologise came from a motor car which had drawn to the side of the pavement precisely opposite Mulberry's shop window. Passers-by who, of course, stopped and stared, had just time to see a face of the very greatest importance against the dove-grey upholstery, before a male hand drew the blind and there was nothing to be seen except a square of dove grey.

No one knows whose face it is, or whether the face and the male hand are parts of the same body, but excited rumors circulate through the streets. Was it the Prince of Wales? The Queen? The Prime Minister? No one knows, but everyone watches from the pavement "with the same dark breath of veneration whether for the Queen, Prince, or Prime Minister nobody knew." The narrator continues on the same theme: "There could be no doubt that greatness was seated within," that the car was bearing "the majesty of England . . . the enduring symbol of the state."

Clarissa, who will later feel something like pity for a Prime Minister in the same room with her, admiringly identifies herself with that symbolic, invisible majesty. She knows it from the inside: "Clarissa guessed; Clarissa knew of course; she had seen something white, magical, circular, in the footman's hand, a disc inscribed with a name,—the Queen's, the Prince of Wales's, the Prime Minister's?" The Queen, Clarissa learned a few moments earlier from an offhand remark by Hugh Whitbread, will be giving a party that night at Buckingham Palace. "And Clarissa, too, gave a party. She stiffened a little; so she would stand at the top of her stairs." Thirty-three years earlier, she had cried in her bedroom remembering Peter Walsh's accusation: "She would marry a Prime Minister and stand at the top of a staircase; the perfect hostess he called her."

The car's movement seems trifling in itself, yet "something had happened . . . in its fulness rather formidable . . . for in all the hat shops and tailors' shops strangers looked at each other and thought of the dead; of the flag; of Empire." A fight breaks out in a pub when someone insults the royal family; in a fashionable club, "Tall men, men of robust physique, well-dressed men" stand straighter, ready to die for their sovereign;* sentries salute; policemen approve.

While the crowds revere the symbol of the state, something else appears that they revere even more and understand even less. A crowd has gathered at the gate of Buckingham Palace waiting for the car to enter. As they wait, they notice an airplane overhead, skywriting—emitting artificial smoke that writes letters in the air. (The first skywriting occurred over London in 1922, a novelty introduced while Virginia Woolf was planning the novel.) Everyone looks up at the white-smoke letters, and everyone has a different, mostly mistaken idea of what the letters are and what they spell out. So when the symbolically weighted royal or official car drives into the Palace, no one notices, because everyone is looking up at the airplane and its writing in the sky.†
In the novel, the car gets only a final parenthesis: "(and the car

---

* The robust, well-dressed men, "for reasons difficult to discriminate, were standing in the bow window of White's," a Tory club. Those reasons had been clear to everyone in the nineteenth century, when the "bow-window at White's" was famous as the vantage point "in which the fashionables sat to show themselves off and to quiz [i.e., ridicule] the passers-by" (thus the 1927 Muirhead's Blue Guide, *London and Its Environs*). In *Mrs. Dalloway* even the fashionables "seemed ready to attend their Sovereign, if need be, to the cannon's mouth, as their ancestors had done before them."

† The car has grey curtains on its windows, but the color of the car itself is never named. Sir William Bradshaw's car, described later in the book, is

went in at the gates and nobody looked at it)." Royalty and empire inspire loyalty and awe, but the triumphant new machine, heralding the information technology of the future and its trivial commercial message—the skywriting seems to be an advertisement for toffee—inspires the crowd even more forcefully to look up at its speed and agility, its freedom, its compelling, evanescent, and mostly incomprehensible message.

Like the car, the airplane inspires more awe as it becomes less visible, less tangible:

> Away and away the aeroplane shot, till it was nothing but a bright spark; an aspiration; a concentration; a symbol (so it seemed to Mr. Bentley, vigourously rolling his strip of turf at Greenwich) of man's soul; of his determination . . . to get outside his body, beyond his house, by means of thought, Einstein, speculation, mathematics, the Mendelian theory . . .

Once again, like the car dissolving into a symbol of the state, the airplane dissolves into a symbol. Here as everywhere in Virginia Woolf's writing, symbols are inherently false: means of evading the unique reality of persons and events—and therefore capable of serving as instruments of anonymous power, all the more effective for being intangible, acting not on the body but on the mind and the soul.

Peter Walsh, returning to England after five years, is a colonial administrator in India, "coming as he did from a respectable Anglo-Indian family [as he thinks to himself] which for at least three generations had administered the affairs of a continent." (Anglo-Indian meant someone of English descent who

---

grey, and both cars have in common the colorlessness of anonymous authority. But only the first car drives into Buckingham Palace.

lived in India; it did not mean someone with one English and one Indian parent.) He has mixed feelings about his imperial role. Early in the book, he finds himself approving English civilization: "Never had he seen London look so enchanting—the softness of the distances; the richness; the greenness; the civilisation, after India, he thought, strolling across the grass."

But the novel also reports him thinking to himself: "it's strange . . . what sentiment I have about that, disliking India, and empire, and army as he did." He has moments of pride about England; he thinks his pride is "ridiculous enough" (his phrase), yet he feels it anyway. And he will feel it again in a deeply ambiguous moment much later in the book, when he hears "the light high bell of the ambulance" and when his pride in England is less self-aware and more thoroughly misplaced.

While walking through London, Peter sees boys of sixteen in uniform marching toward the Cenotaph, the monument to soldiers whose bodies had never been found. The boys "did not look robust," were "weedy for the most part," wearing on their faces "the solemnity of the wreath which they had fetched from Finsbury Pavement to the empty tomb." The social world honors them: "They had taken their vow. The traffic respected it; vans were stopped."

Then the next paragraph recalls another aspect of imperial ambition. Peter stands under the statue of General Charles Gordon, who died in the Sudan as a consequence of his imperial fantasies. Khartoum had been under siege by rebels against the Egyptian government, which was controlled by Britain. Gordon was sent to the Sudan in 1884 with orders to evacuate Khartoum. Instead he fortified the city, but was then unable to break through the siege and escape. After months of dithering, the British government belatedly sent an expeditionary force to relieve him, but he was killed by the rebels before the troops arrived. Gordon died when Peter was around fifteen years old, and he now remembers "Gordon whom as a boy he had worshipped . . . poor Gordon, he thought."

Peter retains a boy's vague image of imperial folly and glory, but a more exact image of the same events is visible a few pages after this, during Lady Bruton's lunch party. The narrator mentions an alcove in Lady Bruton's house with a photograph of a general "who had written there (one evening in the eighties) in Lady Bruton's presence, with her cognisance, perhaps advice, a telegram ordering the British troops to advance upon an historical occasion." What Peter remembers sentimentally, having read about it as a boy, is one of the events in Lady Bruton's personal history that resulted from her status, personality, and power.

The book quietly judges its characters partly on their attitudes toward empire. Clarissa can be rewarded by her moral and psychological revelation at the end partly because she has already glancingly indicated her distaste for the imperial enterprise. Early in the day, puzzled by Peter's eroticism and by his disdain for her prudishness, she thinks: "Never could she understand how he cared. But those Indian women did presumably—silly, pretty, flimsy nincompoops." "Indian women," at the time Virginia Woolf was writing, meant British women living in India as part of colonial society. Clarissa, without being aware of it, is making an anti-imperialist point: the only possible function for wives and daughters in a ruling colonial society is to make themselves decorative.

A TRIUMPH OF CIVILIZATION

The four long paragraphs that tell the personal history of Sir William and Lady Bradshaw—paragraphs that immediately follow the exit of Septimus and Lucrezia from his consulting room—are unlike anything else in the book. The book tells other personal histories—of Septimus, Peter Walsh, Lady Bruton, Miss Kilman, and others—but these four paragraphs about Sir William are the only such histories that seem to have been written in cold fury, and the only ones that extend outward to the social system at its most intense. They move from Sir William himself to the whole enterprise of domination and power, by which he "not only prospered himself but made England prosper." That enterprise culminates in the world-enclosing force of empire—"in the heat and sands of India, the mud and swamp of Africa"—but it also does its work in slums and hospitals.*

Worshipping Proportion, the first of his goddesses, Sir William "not only prospered himself but made England prosper." Then, in the next paragraph, the narrator has this to say about Conversion, the second of Sir William's goddesses, who shares her dominion with his goddess Proportion. Those who worship Conversion include those like Sir William whose worship is rewarded by success, but also those whose worship leads them to a life of resentment and failure, like the tub-thumping ranters at the public speakers' corner in Hyde Park:

> But Proportion has a sister, less smiling, more formidable, a Goddess even now engaged—in the heat and sands of India, the mud and swamp of Africa, the purlieus of London, wherever in short the climate or the devil tempts men to fall from the true belief which is her own. . . . Conversion is her name and she feasts on

---

* The five books that Clarissa sees in Hatchard's window on her morning walk are four that are thoroughly English—a Shakespeare, two comic novels, a memoir by a political wife—and one that looks out toward guns and empire: *Big Game Shooting in Nigeria*. The first four are real; Virginia Woolf invented the fifth.

the wills of the weakly, loving to impress, to impose, adoring her own features stamped on the face of the populace. At Hyde Park Corner on a tub she stands preaching; shrouds herself in white and walks penitentially disguised as brotherly love through factories and parliaments; offers help, but desires power; smites out of her way roughly the dissentient, or dissatisfied; bestows her blessing on those who, looking upward, catch submissively from her eyes the light of their own.

And, the narrator continues, the goddess Conversion, who "loves blood better than brick" in private life as well as in public life, fifteen years ago caused Lady Bradshaw to go under, to sink her will into her husband's will.

When Septimus Warren Smith refuses to submit to the goddess Conversion, her high priest Sir William brings in physical force and the force of law ("he had to support him police and the good of society"*) to enforce the submission she would prefer to be voluntary, and which she almost always gets. Everyone in the book who reveres empire, authority, Englishness, everyone who responds to any of those things even while disliking them, like Peter Walsh "disliking India, and empire, and army," has consented, voluntarily, to Conversion's impersonal power.

Among the many deep connections that Virginia Woolf makes in this novel is the connection between Sir William's goddesses and the archetypal feminine figure in Peter Walsh's dream "who will, with a toss of her head, mount me on her streamers

---

* The phrase "had to support him," meaning that he could rely on support from the police, is the text of the British edition: "There were ... family affection; honour; courage; and a brilliant career. If they failed, he had to support him police ..." An editor of the American edition misinterpreted Virginia Woolf's insertion of "him" in the proofs, and placed the word earlier in the sentence: "If they failed him, he had to support police ..."

and let me blow to nothingness with the rest." Sir William's goddesses are equally mythical figures, but, unlike Peter's myth-figure, they have decisive effects in the real world. The goddess Conversion, by "adoring her own features stamped on the face of the populace," effaces—in the etymological sense of the word—the individual persons who, partly through their submission to her, are subsumed into the generalized face of the populace.

Many varieties of power have a double effect. A civilization, for example, that does unjust harm to those outside it can simultaneously confer real benefits on those inside it: benefits that, for insiders, involve sympathy, generosity, and care. Those who are outsiders to a civilization, like Septimus Warren Smith, may live within its walls, but are exiled from its power and security as firmly as those who live outside its walls in colonial subjection. When Septimus flings himself to his death, he does so in order to evade the power of Sir William Bradshaw—even though the person whose arrival at the door prompts him to jump is Dr. Holmes, who has nothing to do with Sir William. Through the laws that require Septimus to be confined to a mental home because he said he would kill himself, and through the madness provoked by his voluntary war service, he is a victim of the civilization he reveres in the idealized images of Shakespeare and Miss Isabel Pole.

But a few moments after Septimus dies—and a long section of the book that focused on Septimus comes to an end—the tone of the book changes. The next section begins by focusing on Peter Walsh as he walks to his hotel:

> One of the triumphs of civilisation, Peter Walsh thought. It is one of the triumphs of civilisation, as the light high bell of the ambulance sounded. Swiftly, cleanly, the ambulance sped to the

hospital, having picked up instantly, humanely, some poor devil; some one hit on the head, struck down by disease, knocked over perhaps a minute or so ago at one of these crossings, as might happen to oneself. That was civilisation. It struck him coming back from the East—the efficiency, the organisation, the communal spirit of London. Every cart or carriage of its own accord drew aside to let the ambulance pass.

This paragraph seems to me devastating and heartbreaking—and not only because the world it describes, with its communal spirit, has long since disappeared. What Peter says about civilization is true: the ambulance's swift passage through the crowded streets is a great triumph of civilization; and the whole passage echoes the pleasure that Virginia Woolf recorded in her diary after moving house from suburban Richmond to central London in 1924. ("London is enchanting . . . , how it takes up the private life and carries it on, without any effort.") What is also true is that Septimus, the victim toward whom the ambulance is hurrying in the hope of bringing aid, was struck down by that civilization, precisely as a consequence of his choice to defend it.

Virginia Woolf seems to make in this passage a gentle but decisive moral rebuke to her friend E. M. Forster, who had recently written a similar moment into his novel *A Passage to India* (1924). Forster described an Englishman returning from India to Europe who is delighted to get back to "the civilization that has escaped muddle"—and Forster wrote this entirely without irony, as if "muddle" (one of Forster's recurring terms of disapproval), not cruelty or oppression, was the problem that civilization exists in order to solve.

The truth that Virginia Woolf expresses in Peter's thoughts about the ambulance is the truth that every civilization, no matter how just, creates victims. This truth does not imply the relativist fantasy that societies and cultures must not be subject to judgment because all are unjust, the fantasy that all moral distinctions are relative. (If you can't tell the difference between, say, the Aztec culture of human sacrifice and the monastic culture of Tibet, then you need to start attending to reality.) But this truth does mean that every time you draw a glass of water from the faucet, every time you walk down a lighted sidewalk, you enjoy the benefits of a civilization that unjustly harms someone else. And the relative merit of a merely moderately unjust society doesn't mean much to the person with the bad fortune to be excluded from it, or beaten up in it, or killed by its agents. W. H. Auden wrote in a prose poem: "without a cement of blood (it must be human, it must be innocent), no secular wall will safely stand."

THE OPPRESSED WHO OPPRESSES

A variation on this theme in *Mrs. Dalloway* is that it is not only successful insiders, not only Sir William Bradshaw and Lady Bruton, who wield power over others. The weak and powerless do the same, or try to. Readers do not need to be taught that the physical and social forces that gather to confine Septimus Warren Smith in a mental home are unjust. What a great and disturbing novel like this one can point to, however, are the ways in which the victims of power can also wield power cruelly or selfishly, can become empire-builders in the personal realm because they are excluded from the political one.

Doris Kilman, Elizabeth's private tutor, is unambiguously a victim of injustice, someone who did nothing to deserve having been victimized by the same national and imperial pressures that made a victim of Septimus Warren Smith. Miss Kilman's family was originally German (they spelled it Kiehlman in the eighteenth century); she had German friends; "the only happy days of her life had been spent in Germany!" In the 1914–1918 War more or less everyone in England decided it was obligatory to hate all Germans, but Miss Kilman "had never been able to tell lies." Her brother was an English soldier killed in battle—like Clarissa she has lost a sibling, like Septimus she has lost a loved one in war—but she refused to say that she hated all Germans, and so she was fired by the girls' school where she had been teaching and could never again find a regular job.

Bitter, resentful, knowing she had been treated unjustly, she now scrapes together a living giving extension lectures (like Miss Pole lecturing on Shakespeare) and tutoring Elizabeth Dalloway, and through the Rev. Edward Whittaker she has found in religion a justification for her bitterness:

> She had seen the light two years and three months ago. Now she did not envy women like Clarissa Dalloway; she pitied them.
> She pitied and despised them from the bottom of her heart. . . . She had heard the Rev. Edward Whittaker preach; the boys sing; had seen the solemn lights descend. . . . So now, whenever the hot and painful feelings boiled within her, this hatred of Mrs. Dalloway, this grudge against the world, she thought of God.

But she forgets God in the offending presence of Clarissa, when her *libido dominandi* surges within her: "there rose in her [Miss Kilman] an overmastering desire to overcome her [Clarissa]; to unmask her. If she could have felled her it would have eased her. But it was not the body; it was the soul and its mockery that she wished to subdue; make feel her mastery."

As Auden wrote in an ironic song, "Many a sore bottom finds / A sorer one to kick." Miss Kilman's family name, like

Lady Bruton's, is one of Virginia Woolf's rare signals of a character through a name.

The point of the symmetry between Miss Kilman and Septimus Warren Smith—each living in the world of extension lectures, each with a brother or brother-in-arms killed in the war—is to emphasize the different responses that can be provoked by being cruelly wronged: Miss Kilman's bitterness, Septimus's suicide. Unjust oppression does not make her virtuous or noble in her suffering, in the way that much of sentimental culture and literature imagines it can. She too, like Sir William Bradshaw, worships the goddess Conversion. She persuades Elizabeth to join her in prayer; she wants Elizabeth to join in her contempt for Clarissa. What she feels toward Elizabeth is a love that wants absolute possession: "If she [Miss Kilman] could grasp her, if she could clasp her, if she could make her hers absolutely and for ever and then die; that was all she wanted.* But to sit here, unable to think of anything to say; to see Elizabeth turning against her; to be felt repulsive even by her—it was too much; she could not stand it."

A few pages later, when she is praying in Westminster Abbey for relief from her angers, a well-dressed man in the same row is at first "a little distressed by the poor lady's disorder," but is then impressed by "her largeness, robustness, and power"—as Clarissa, the Rev. Edward Whittaker, and Elizabeth have also been impressed. Virginia Woolf takes great care when describing characters as having an inherent power, power

---

* This is close to Clarissa's thought many years ago about Sally Seton: "feeling as she crossed the hall 'if it were now to die 'twere now to be most happy.' That was her feeling—Othello's feeling, and she felt it, she was convinced, as strongly as Shakespeare meant Othello to feel it . . ." And in the little room at her party, she remembers that feeling: " 'If it were now to die,'twere now to be most happy,' she had said to herself once, coming down in white."

within themselves, not merely power over someone else. This is not simply a matter of rank. Sir William Bradshaw, Lady Bruton, and Miss Kilman all have that kind of power. The Prime Minister does not.

Many readers who know better can still take pleasure in pious fictions that divide the world into wicked oppressors and innocent victims: novels and films that contrast the oppressor's brutal culture with the victim's innocent arcadia. The film *Avatar* (2009) is one of the clearest recent examples: the individualistic high-tech oppressors from Earth are the exact moral opposite of the instinctive, empathetic tribe on a distant primitive planet. For the naïve, to suggest anything other than this sharp contrast would seem to justify oppression, or at least make excuses for it.

The falsehood that drives *Avatar*, and all fictions that share its assumptions, is the premise that oppression is bad *because* its victims are innocent. This is both morally wrong and intellectually incoherent. Oppression is evil both when its victims are corrupt and debased and when they are innocent and noble. Morally, it is the act that matters, not the character of those who are acted upon. What is not merely false but also pernicious about the *Avatar* model of justice is that it invites its audience to enjoy the fantasy that they are right to oppress their own enemies because, in their eyes, those enemies are not innocent, that those they hate deserve to be oppressed. And once this fantasy gets into the head of anyone convinced of their own virtue, it is almost impossible to dislodge.

James Joyce's politics in *Ulysses* conforms to this fantasy, and in a simpleminded way. The book treats national politics as a variety of family politics, different in scale, not in kind, with the patriarchal British oppressing the childishly feckless Irish, who at worst are mildly prejudiced against Jews but are never tempted to oppression, not even capable of it.

Virginia Woolf gets these matters right. In her daily life and in her nonfictional prose she held strong views about national and sexual politics; she took sides, always in complex, self-doubting ways. But in her novels, she did not take sides, instead doing something more subtle—and she seems to have done this as a conscious decision, after having tried and failed to write fiction that took sides in the way her nonfictional prose did.* She began her late novel *The Years* (1937) by drafting it, under the title *The Pargiters*, as an experimental hybrid in which expository political essays alternated with the chapters of fiction. Then she rewrote and published it with only the fiction, and with no explicit politics. The politics of Virginia Woolf's nonfictional work seems to me wholly admirable, and so does the lack of politics in her fictional work.

First, her politics, as they exist outside her fiction. She was mostly conflicted about the value of collective action, but she was, for much of her life, emphatically feminist (although reluctant to be labeled as such),† emphatically pacifist, and more or less sympathetic with the least militant wing of the Labour Party, a wing that was very much in the party's minority. She admired her husband's moral and civic values, but was far less interested than he was in political action. As she wrote in her

---

* Günter Grass once told an audience that whenever he began writing something about politics he knew how it would come out; whenever he began writing a novel he had no idea how it would come out.

† She wrote in her diary, "if I were still a feminist.... But I have travelled on" (17 October 1924); she wrote in a letter, "if I were a feminist" (to Ethel Smyth, 15 April 1931). Her books *A Room of One's Own* (1929) and *Three Guineas* (1938) are deeply feminist, but she rejected a possible title for *Three Guineas* ("Men are like that") as "too patently feminist" (diary, 16 February 1932). She seems to have assigned a specific meaning to *feminist* that differed from the more common ones.

diary: "L. and I quarrelled last night. I dislike the tub thumper in him; he the irrational Xtian [Christian] in me."*

In the broadest sense, her politics were close to the liberal left (with a lowercase "l" in both words), I think because the liberal left, despite its faults, prejudices, blindnesses, and errors, was (and remains) the only variety of politics that felt obliged to care more or less equally about, on the one hand, individual freedom, and on the other hand, mutual responsibility. In this, the liberal left differs from the anarchist left and libertarian right who imagine it is morally and practically possible to have freedom without responsibility, and differs also from the moralizing left and the authoritarian right who imagine that people can be coerced, without freedom, into mutual responsibility. These other ways of thinking are adolescent fantasies about adolescent politics, fantasies that seem plausible only if you know nothing about your inner life and its relation to other people's lives. Virginia Woolf knew everything about the inner life, and her politics were adult.

She had a strong sense that an artist's politics could not be partisan, but must be simultaneously unique to the individual and potentially suitable for everyone. In an essay on art and politics that she published in the *Daily Worker*—the Communist editors cordoned it off with a note saying they didn't "entirely" agree with it—she wrote: "the practice of art, far from making the artist out of touch with his kind, rather [i.e., instead] increases his sensibility. It breeds in him a feeling for the passions and needs of mankind in the mass which the citizen whose duty it is

---

* Both these figures seem to be combined in one of the avatars of Sir William Bradshaw's goddess Conversion: "At Hyde Park Corner on a tub she stands preaching."

to work for a particular country or for a particular party has no time and perhaps no need to cultivate."

And when she wrote about collective political activity in a preface to a book of memoirs published by a working women's guild, she saw the purpose of collective action to be the liberation of individual lives: "the women would cease to be symbols," she wrote, "and would become instead individuals."

That, briefly, is the politics of her nonfictional prose. Her fiction, although driven forcefully by her sense of justice and injustice, seems to have no partisan politics at all. One striking detail of *Mrs. Dalloway* is that Clarissa's husband Richard is a Conservative member of Parliament—exactly the sort of person whom Virginia Woolf mostly disdained in her life outside her fiction. (In Britain in 1925, "Conservative" meant something not entirely unlike what "Liberal" means now. That is, a Conservative could think that justice can be achieved without changing the social order, while a member of the Liberal or Labour parties assumed that social change was a prerequisite for justice.) Virginia Woolf, despite her extrafictional politics, made Richard Dalloway the only character in the book who cares about justice; and he cares about it in morally admirable ways.*

Richard works on a parliamentary committee in aid of Armenian refugees. (Clarissa can never remember if they are Armenian or Albanian.) His mental vocabulary is simplistic, but his sense of "the social system . . . at its most intense" is as strong as his author's: "He had no illusions about the London police.

---

* As in *Between the Acts*, where the stockbroker Giles Oliver, with his angry sexual prejudices, is the only character who notices and despises Nazi murderousness and, in June 1939, foresees and dreads the coming war.

Indeed, he was collecting evidence of their malpractices; and those costermongers, not allowed to stand their barrows in the streets; and prostitutes, good Lord, the fault wasn't in them, nor in young men either, but in our detestable social system and so forth . . ."

He thinks in clichés; Peter Walsh can't bear to hear his philistine platitudes about Shakespeare. At Bourton years ago, "solemnly Richard Dalloway got on his hind legs and said that no decent man ought to read Shakespeare's sonnets because it was like listening at keyholes." But Richard has absolutely no prejudice against Miss Kilman of the kind that Clarissa has: "Richard said she was very able, had a really historical mind." And he shares, inarticulately, Clarissa's distaste for Sir William Bradshaw: he "didn't like his taste, didn't like his smell." The novel refuses to judge his ethical merits by his vocabulary, his literary sensibility, or his party affiliation.

Virginia Woolf's sexual politics are equally complex and judicious. Her nonfiction includes *A Room of One's Own* and *Three Guineas*, each in turn the greatest feminist polemic in English since Mary Wollstonecraft, and in these books and in her essays she wrote in praise of women acting in affiliation, acting together in a common cause. But all this is absent from her fiction, and her fiction is deeply skeptical of categories of human beings united for a single purpose. *Mrs. Dalloway* emphasizes how manipulative it is—and how deeply in service to power—to invite others to join you in a shared purpose based on a sexual category or any other shared identity. The narrator's habitual irony about anyone named Lady Something sharpens its edge when Lady Bruton signals "recognition of some feminine comradeship" or when Lady Bradshaw—whose whole existence is a lie—lowers her voice in a wheedling way, "drawing Mrs. Dalloway into the shelter of a common femininity" (and Lady Bradshaw thinks of her as Mrs. Dalloway, not Clarissa). Of all the characters in the book, it is only these corrupt figures who think about a common femininity.

LADY BEXBOROUGH AND THE REST OF IT

Virginia Woolf returned to the temptations of "a common femininity" in her next novel, *To the Lighthouse*, where Mrs. Ramsay wants everyone to let their lives be shaped by categories. Categories give her a sense of her own powers of benevolent control: "Indeed, she had the whole of the other sex under her protection; for reasons she could not explain, for their chivalry and valour, for the fact that they negotiated treaties, ruled India, controlled finance..." Her children's "infidel ideas" of lives uniquely their own seem to her deplorable: "It seemed to her such nonsense—inventing differences, when people, heaven knows, were different enough without that. The real differences, she thought, ... are enough, quite enough. She had in mind at the moment, rich and poor, high and low..."

And she hopes she might someday work to understand, not individual suffering, but the social problems of England that Sir William works to solve, in the hope that she could "become what with her untrained mind she greatly admired, an investigator, elucidating the social problem."

When Lady Bradshaw invites Clarissa to share in a common femininity, she is tempting her to sacrifice personal freedom for the sake of an imaginary purpose. Clarissa yields repeatedly to this temptation, especially when she thinks about her parties.

She worries a great deal about having been pressured by a friend to invite her impoverished cousin Ellie Henderson to her party: "why should she invite all the dull women in London to her parties?" Richard, she knows, "did not see the reasons against asking Ellie Henderson": he "had no notion of the look of a room." He makes moral judgments where she makes aesthetic ones. And when Clarissa agrees to invite Ellie because Richard wishes it, "why did she suddenly feel, for no reason that she could discover, desperately unhappy?" Appearances, and other people's imagined judgments, to her mean everything.

At the end, the novel tells the story of Clarissa's education out of this self-defeating error. That education takes place at her party, and it can take place nowhere else, because only in the midst of her party, having placed her hopes in it, can she learn how unsatisfying, how delusory, those hopes are. At first the party seems to satisfy all her wishes. She thrills at the arrival of the Prime Minister, a lion-hunting hostess's greatest possible catch, short of the royal family, and enjoys the pleasure of escorting him around the room, even though she sees that the Prime Minister is, personally, nobody. She enjoys the pleasure of being envied, the pleasure of knowing what other people feel. Then her pleasure evaporates the moment the Prime Minister starts to leave:

> Indeed, Clarissa felt, the Prime Minister had been good to come. And, walking down the room with him . . . with all those people rather inclined, perhaps, to envy, she had felt that intoxication of the moment . . . ; yes, but after all it was what other people felt, that; for, though she loved it and felt it tingle and sting, still these semblances, these triumphs . . . had a hollowness; at arm's length they were, not in the heart; and it might be that she was growing old, but they satisfied her no longer as they used . . .

She has now seen that the power she worships is trivial and empty, that its unsatisfying "semblances"* are not real, not in the heart; "after all it was what other people felt." But instead of feeling anger at herself for worshiping false gods, instead of feeling anger at the false gods themselves, she clings to the world of power and hierarchy by finding someone else, someone weaker, to feel angry at. As she sees the Prime Minister descend the stairs, something irrelevant in her line of vision, the gilt rim of a picture frame, somehow "suddenly" evokes the object of anger that she needs. The gilt rim "brought back Kilman with a rush; Kilman her enemy. That was satisfying; that was real. Ah, how she hated her—hot, hypocritical, corrupt; with all that power; Elizabeth's seducer; the woman who had crept in to steal and defile. . . . It was enemies one wanted, not friends . . ."

In the next stage of Clarissa's education, she will stop looking to someone else for comfort, either through enhancing her pride with praise or through providing an object to blame, and instead confront herself. That stage begins a few pages later, when she enters the little room where the Prime Minister and Lady Bruton had been talking about India and sees that "there was nobody." In the emptiness of the little room, as she senses with uncanny accuracy that Septimus had killed himself rather than submit to the power embodied in Sir William Bradshaw, she also senses her own willing submission to that same power in its other forms, her deferent complicity in a world of power relations, status and envy, a world without sympathy or love. "It was her punishment to see sink and disappear here a man, there a

---

* The uncommon word "semblance" occurs in seven of Virginia Woolf's novels and many of her essays, typically meaning something that appears to be the case but isn't.

woman, in this profound darkness, and she forced to stand here in her evening dress."

She knows how much she has wanted the kinds of power that express themselves as status, as success: "She had schemed; she had pilfered [pilfered what? perhaps other people's phrases or gossip?]. She was never wholly admirable. She had wanted success, Lady Bexborough and the rest of it. And once she had walked on the terrace at Bourton."

The novel compresses a whole psychology of envy, ambition, and status-worship into Clarissa's quick contemptuous phrase, "Lady Bexborough and the rest of it,"* followed by another compressed phrase about an entirely different psychology of feeling and exaltation: "And once she had walked on the terrace at Bourton." There, at eighteen, she had been kissed by Sally Seton and felt "the revelation, the religious feeling!"

Another phrase in this passage, also a triumph of psychological compression, deserves a closer second look: "and she forced to stand here in her evening dress." In the world of power relations that Clarissa imagines around her, all her actions seem to her to have been shaped by power. But no one but herself has ever forced Clarissa to stand here in her evening dress. No one forces her to give her parties; no one even wants her to give them. Her husband is puzzled that she cares about them: "it was a very odd thing how much Clarissa minded about her parties, he thought. . . . If she worried about these parties he would not let her give them." Peter Walsh, as she knows, is infuriated by them. Her daughter is bored by them and wishes she could be

---

* In the British edition, quoted here, a comma separates "She had wanted success" and "Lady Bexborough and the rest of it." The American edition, apparently in error, has a full stop. The proofs, like the British edition, have a comma, but in the first set of proofs (for her friend Jacques Raverat) Virginia Woolf added a dash after the comma to emphasize the break.

somewhere else with her dog. The only person who seems to enjoy the party, because she can tell someone else about it, is Ellie Henderson, whom Clarissa didn't want there at all.*

Only two paragraphs earlier, Clarissa had used the word "force" in a superficially different sense, when she thought of Sir William Bradshaw as "capable of... forcing your soul." The forcing that Sir William does is real and fatal; but when Clarissa thinks of herself as "forced to stand here in her evening dress," she is granting power to something unreal, something that she invents and to which she then insists on yielding.

Clarissa alone invents the imperative to give a party and stand there in her evening dress—Clarissa alone who, in her own words, "had wanted success." She told herself, a few hours before, that she is not a snob who wants famous people around her, as Peter thinks, or that she has a childish wish for excitement, as Richard thinks: "both were quite wrong," she says. "What she liked was simply life. 'That's what I do it for,' she said, speaking aloud, to life."

Power is everywhere in this novel, and Virginia Woolf has no fantasy that personal or political acts can end its dominion. But she combined her exact attention to the state of the present with an imaginative vision of an apocalyptic future when everything will change. While she was writing *Mrs. Dalloway* she also wrote a brief essay on the British Empire Exhibition at Wembley in 1924, an exhibition that explicitly celebrated "the imperial idea." Her essay is a fantasia on the future disintegration of the exhibition, and on the future disintegration of empire, by forces

---

* It is something of a critical commonplace that Clarissa gives her parties because her culture requires her to perform "women's work." This is not the case, although Clarissa imagines something like it until, at the party, she sees through her mistake.

of nature that rain in from the sky because the exhibition site was open to the air. The essay ends: "The Empire is perishing; the bands are playing; the Exhibition is in ruins. For that is what comes of letting in the sky." The same apocalyptic idea occurs early in *Mrs. Dalloway* when, as the motor car moves through the streets, the narrator suddenly imagines a distant future, in "the ruins of time," when the majesty of England has disintegrated in imperial apocalypse, and "London is a grass-grown path" with nothing left of its citizens but the dust of their bones, their innumerable gold fillings, and a few wedding rings.

In the last pages of the book, after Clarissa comes in from the little room to find Sally Seton and Peter Walsh, the book itself has changed. It is no longer a story about power, but about something else that has something to do with those wedding rings in the dust. In the very last lines of the book, Peter Walsh experiences something outside himself that affects him deeply, not in the way that power affects anyone, but with the terror and ecstasy that fill him with his sense of "Clarissa herself." Earlier in the day, Clarissa had wondered about a similar moment of ecstasy long ago, on the terrace at Bourton when she was kissed by Sally and experienced "the revelation, the religious feeling!" Now, three decades later, she meditates on "this question of love" and asks herself about her adolescent ecstasy: "Had not that, after all, been love?" My first two chapters have been about the question of power; the third will be about what Virginia Woolf had to say about that perennial, urgent "question of love."

3

LOVE

"But this question of love (she thought, putting her coat away)..." Clarissa thinks about this open question early in the June day chronicled in *Mrs. Dalloway*. Everyone else, at some point later in the day, also faces that question.*

When W. H. Auden arrived in America from England in 1939 he wrote to a friend back home that he very much liked his new country even though, he said, "Americans always want answers to everything, and when you tell them there aren't any, are very upset." Virginia Woolf had no answer to the question of love, nor to any other urgent question, but in *Mrs. Dalloway* her inconclusive thoughts about it are clarifying and invigorating in ways that attempts at answers can't be.

Clarissa starts thinking about love in the fifth paragraph of the book, when she starts her day by congratulating herself for loving life, for loving the London scene:

---

* As does Lily Briscoe in *To the Lighthouse*, when, puzzled by the erotic excitement provoked in her by Paul Rayley, she attends to the talk around the table at Mrs. Ramsay's dinner party: "So she listened again to what they were saying in case they should throw any light upon the question of love." What she hears, however, is Mr. Bankes inveighing against "that liquid the English call coffee."

> For Heaven only knows why one loves it so, how one sees it so . . . the veriest frumps, the most dejected of miseries sitting on doorsteps . . . they love life. In people's eyes, in the swing, tramp, and trudge . . . in the triumph and the jingle and the strange high singing of some aeroplane overhead was what she loved; life; London; this moment of June.

And a few pages later she praises herself again: "what she loved was this, here, now, in front of her; the fat lady in the cab."

Then, in the next sentence, she wonders, "did it matter that she must inevitably cease completely." This is the first of many moments when thoughts of love and death crowd in on each other, when someone uses thoughts about love as a defense against the realities of death. It is still too early in the book, and too early in the day, for Clarissa to see the deep connection between love and mortality, or to ask whether her love for the fat lady in the cab could possibly matter to the lady, or to herself, or to anyone at all.

Peter Walsh has returned from India to London to arrange a divorce for the twenty-four-year-old Englishwoman whom he wants to marry, while still in love with Clarissa, as he always has been. Thirty-three years earlier she broke his heart by rejecting him and marrying Richard Dalloway instead, even though—as her friends could see at the time—she was still in love with Peter. She half recognizes that she married Richard *because* she was in love with Peter, because the emotional intimacy of a marriage with Peter would have been too much for her to face. Richard Dalloway, for all his kindness and virtue, has never asked her for emotional intimacy; he scarcely seems to know what it might be. Peter, meanwhile, after losing Clarissa, married, on the rebound, a woman he met on the boat to India. And now, having divorced that wife, he is planning, not very enthusiastically, to marry a second wife whom he met while living in India.

Peter and Clarissa both spend much of the day trying to convince themselves that they are better off as they are:

> [Clarissa is] still making out that she had been right—and she had too—not to marry him. For in marriage, a little licence, a little independence there must be between people living together day in day out in the same house; which Richard gave her, and she him. . . . But with Peter everything had to be shared; everything gone into. . . . [S]he had to break with him or they would have been destroyed, both of them ruined, she was convinced; though she had borne about with her for years like an arrow sticking in her heart the grief, the anguish . . .

Peter has spent the past thirty-three years, having lost Clarissa, trying to console himself by attaching himself to women who offer the comfort of sex. He keeps complaining to himself that Clarissa refuses intimacy, that she retains something of the manner that annoyed him when she was a girl: "timid; hard; arrogant; prudish." If Clarissa had married him, he tells himself, "it would not have been a success, their marriage. The other thing, after all, came so much more naturally." The "other thing" is sex, which is what his intended second wife Daisy promised him when she ran across the veranda, indifferent to anyone who might be looking, and cried out: "she would give him everything . . . everything he wanted!" Peter, Daisy thinks, "was a man. But not the sort of man one had to respect—which was a mercy, not like Major Simmons [her husband], for instance; not in the least, Daisy thought, when in spite of her two small children, she used to compare them." The respect required by Major Simmons gets in the way of intimacy; Peter, mercifully, was a man who requires nothing of that.

In a book that names a dozen or more varieties of unconscious, gatherable flowers—"delphiniums, sweet peas, bunches of lilac; and carnations . . . roses . . . irises"—Daisy is the only character who is named for one. She can give Peter everything he wants except what he will always want, which is Clarissa. Yet what Peter feels toward Clarissa is not quite *wanting*. The narrator provides glimpses of what he feels by listening in as he thinks again and again about her. At one point, he starts by focusing on her merits: she is "a far better judge of character" than their friend Sally Seton. And this is something that can be judged more or less objectively. Clarissa is in fact a shrewd judge of character; she senses, for example, the obscure evil in Sir William Bradshaw. But Peter then thinks about something that isn't objective—what he calls Clarissa's "extraordinary gift, that woman's gift, of making a world of her own wherever she happened to be."

Peter never realizes that Clarissa's extraordinary gift—"that woman's gift"—exists only for him.* It never occurs to anyone else that she has that gift. Peter sees Clarissa making a world of her own because he is in love with her: "She came into a room [he remembers]; she stood, as he had often seen her, in a doorway with lots of people round her. But it was Clarissa one remembered. Not that she was striking; not beautiful at all; there was nothing picturesque about her; she never said anything specially clever; there she was, however; there she was."

---

  * Augustine wrote (in Henry Chadwick's free rendering in his *Augustine*, 1986): "Adam did not love Eve because she was beautiful; it was his love which made her beautiful." Somewhat more literally: "The bridegroom [Adam] did not love a bride who was beautiful, but in order to make her beautiful" (*Exposition on Psalm 132*).

She isn't striking or beautiful or clever; he doesn't love her for any of these things; he loves her for being Clarissa. But in his next thought he tries to deny this. "No, no, no!" he thinks. "He was not in love with her any more!" And he keeps insisting he is not in love with her. The fact that he can't stop thinking about her, he tells himself, "was not being in love, of course; it was thinking of her, criticising her . . . trying to explain her."

At one point early in the day, he hears the bells of St. Margaret's Church chiming the hour, and he feels the sound gliding into his heart, "like something alive," he thinks, "which wants to confide itself, to disperse itself, to be, with a tremor of delight, at rest—like Clarissa herself, thought Peter Walsh." And he now realizes what had affected him when the hour sounded: "It is Clarissa herself, he thought, with a deep emotion, and an extraordinarily clear, yet puzzling, recollection of her . . ."

"Clarissa herself" is what he calls her, twice, and this phrase says much about the way he loves her. Virginia Woolf thought deeply in *Mrs. Dalloway* and elsewhere about the connections between love and self, and what she said about those two ideas is worth pausing over.

Today's culture is not much different from hers in its tendencies toward caution and mistrust about the whole idea of unique individual selves, an idea that has been shaken for more than a century by the joint heritage of Freud, Marx, Weber, and many more. In some corners of today's culture, an individual point of view and a clear sense of self are liable to be taken as intellectually irresponsible, in conflict with objectivity and professionalism, something abrasive at best, aggressive at worst. Pressure is subtly felt to perceive oneself as belonging to some generational or specialist category, some field membership, some collective identity. Sooner or later, almost everyone, it sometimes seems, wants to speak *as* a member of some category (or, more aggressively, *for* some category): *as* a scientist, *as* a parent, *as* a theoretician, not wanting or daring, at least for the moment, to speak for oneself.

Virginia Woolf's phrase about "the difficult business of intimacy" points toward the reality that category-thinking denies. However abrasive or aggressive or annoying it may be, only a unique self can achieve intimacy, can make some deep connection with someone else. The self has rough surfaces, but a rough surface gives another self something to hold on to. It is easier to dissolve into some collective identity, where all rough differences can be smoothed out, than to attempt the difficult business of intimacy—but far less satisfying, and far less practical as a way to lead one's life.*

Virginia Woolf had sharp things to say about the fear of being oneself and of speaking for oneself. She wrote about what she called "real people . . . of an unreal type": that is, people who choose to be unreal by dissolving themselves into a type, by adopting a group identity. She was writing about the people you overhear in a café talking slang. They talk slang, she said, "because slang is the speech of the herd, seemingly much at their ease, and yet if we look at them a little from the shadow not at their ease at all, and, indeed, terribly afraid of being

---

* Virginia Woolf of course had no fantasy that the self remains the same, or that everyone has only one self. For example, she wrote in her diary: "I am trying to tell whichever self it is that reads this hereafter that I can write very much better . . ." (20 April 1919). And Orlando, in the novel named for her, has as many as "two thousand" selves. Something like a central, single self exists, but it eludes any attempt to find it. It is only when Orlando is distracted from herself, when she stops seeking among her many selves the "Captain self, the Key self, which amalgamates and controls them all," that she can become "what is called, rightly or wrongly, a single self, a real self."

themselves, or they would say things simply in their natural voices."*

The "soul, or life within us," she wrote in her essay on Montaigne, "is always saying the very opposite to what other people say."

"Terribly afraid of being themselves": what frustrates Peter about Clarissa is her refusal to be "Clarissa herself," the Clarissa he loves. He blames her for insisting instead on being the "perfect hostess" at the top of her stairs—as in fact she is proud to be at the top of her stairs, hostess of her party.

Early in the book, when Clarissa withdraws to her room "like a nun withdrawing, or a child exploring a tower," she has some interesting thoughts about the self. She is thinking about her emotional isolation, her erotic coldness, what the narrator calls "a virginity preserved through childbirth which clung to her like a sheet." (And these are the exact things that Peter blames her for.) She remembers an episode early in her marriage to Richard when, "through some contraction of this cold spirit, she had failed him," failed him in erotic intimacy, and now, "could see what she lacked . . . something central which permeated." This is an exact description of the self that exists at a person's center and that permeates into relations with other selves.

Clarissa tries to explain how it happened: "She resented it, had a scruple picked up Heaven knows where, or, as she felt, sent by Nature (who is invariably wise) . . ." Clarissa's feeling that her coldness had been imposed on her by Nature is especially striking, I think, because morally and intellectually it is the same

---

* On the fear of being oneself. Talking with a doctoral student at a humanities institute, I referred to Virginia Woolf as a genius. The student, nervously: "But of course *we* [we professional academics] don't believe in genius any longer." I: "*We* don't believe in it, but do *you*, personally, believe in it?" The student, brightly: "Of course I do. Doesn't everyone?"

neurobiological fallacy that I mentioned earlier—the fallacy that makes use of something impersonal, chemical, biological, natural, to explain your unhappiness, and not something like that moment long ago when Clarissa's sister Sylvia was killed by a falling tree, killed by paternal incompetence.

Clarissa, in her own way, is "terribly afraid" of being herself. She has perfected a defensive habit of backing away from any sense that she herself performed some action. Instead, she attributes her act to something impersonal outside herself, just as she does when she thinks of her coldness as a scruple sent by Nature. In the same few minutes when she thinks about that coldness, she takes down her green dress to repair it, and this is what goes through her mind: "She had torn it. Some one had trod on the skirt. She had felt it give at the Embassy party at the top among the folds."

These three sentences are quiet expressions of Virginia Woolf's psychological genius. What Clarissa thinks first is that "she had torn it," that she, Clarissa, tore the dress. Then she backs away from this thought, and her next sentence blames someone else: "Some one had trod on the skirt." And then, in the third sentence, it turns out that no one had done anything at all: "She had felt it give at the Embassy party." Two selves, first her own, then someone else's, have been made to disappear.

LOVE AND RELIGION

Every time Clarissa draws away from her sense of self, she evades something that Peter Walsh, when he thinks about "Clarissa herself," senses about the self and about love. She has many ways of evading it.

Early in the book, she puzzles over the connection between her daughter Elizabeth and Elizabeth's tutor, the victimized and repellent Miss Kilman, who sits with Elizabeth over a prayer book, who wants Elizabeth to join her in church. "It might be only a phase," Clarissa thinks, "as Richard said, such as all girls go through. It might be falling in love. But why with Miss Kilman?"

Later, seeing them go out together, Elizabeth well-dressed, Miss Kilman in her shabby mackintosh, Clarissa erupts in inward fury at Miss Kilman's emotional and religious possessiveness toward Elizabeth:

> Love and religion! thought Clarissa . . . tingling all over. How destestable [sic], how detestable they are!* . . . The cruellest things in the world, she thought, seeing them clumsy, hot, domineering, hypocritical, eavesdropping, jealous, infinitely cruel and unscrupulous dressed in a mackintosh coat . . . love and religion. Had she [Clarissa] ever tried to convert any one herself? Did she not wish everybody merely to be themselves?

She is probably flattering herself—she does wish everybody to be themselves while she also wishes not to have any contact with their selves—but she is not wrong about Miss Kilman. Miss Kilman, defeated by other people's power, now wants power for herself. I quoted earlier the passage in which Miss Kilman wishes to subdue Clarissa's "soul and its mockery . . . make feel her mastery." Clarissa senses in Miss Kilman the same dominating will that she senses in Sir William Bradshaw when she thinks him "capable of some indescribable outrage—forcing your soul" and

---

* A note on p. 109 discusses Virginia Woolf's conflicting orthography in this sentence.

the same dominating will that drives Sir William's goddess Conversion, who "feasts on the wills of the weakly," who "walks penitentially disguised as brotherly love." In her moment of fury, Clarissa can think of love only as a disguise worn by that power-thirsty goddess.* She is equally furious at the erotic love that drives Peter Walsh to the vulgar women he marries: "Horrible passion! she thought. Degrading passion! she thought, thinking of Kilman and her Elizabeth . . ."

While Clarissa fumes over Peter, Elizabeth, and Miss Kilman, she notices the old woman in the house opposite, walking upstairs, unaware of being seen, secure in her privacy. Clarissa justifies her anger by telling herself that all she wants is to respect the privacy of the old woman's self, the privacy of everyone's self. She calls it "the privacy of the soul." "There was something solemn in it," she says, something that "love and religion would destroy."

For Clarissa, here and everywhere in the book until almost the end, anything that breaks through the privacy of the soul is destructive, something to avoid in others and repress in herself. Her whole experience of emotional intimacy with Peter, the intimacy she repressed thirty-three years ago, has left her permanently wounded. As she says of their breakup, "she had borne about with her for years like an arrow sticking in her heart the grief, the anguish."

But Peter Walsh has no idea that Clarissa feels this or anything else: "Clarissa was as cold as an icicle." And he generalizes, "women . . . don't know what passion is. They don't know

---

* Clarissa seems to fear that Elizabeth has something of the same feelings toward Miss Kilman (they pray together) that Clarissa felt at eighteen for Sally Seton. But Elizabeth is tolerantly bored by Miss Kilman, nothing more.

the meaning of it to men." But Peter is wrong. Clarissa represses her feelings toward him and others; they can emerge only after an inner struggle; but those feelings are real. During Peter's morning visit, she arms herself for the war between the sexes: "So before a battle begins, the horses paw the ground; toss their heads; the light shines on their flanks; their necks curve. So Peter Walsh and Clarissa, sitting side by side on the blue sofa, challenged each other."

Each wields a sexually appropriate weapon. He annoys her by opening and shutting his pocketknife: "For Heaven's sake, leave your knife alone! she cried to herself in irrepressible irritation." When he shuts his knife with a snap, Clarissa, two sentences later, "opened her scissors." But this is a lovers' quarrel that renews love. After a few more sentences, Peter, running his finger along his knife, thinks with childish resentment, "I'll show Clarissa"—when suddenly their battle ends:

> he burst into tears; wept; wept without the least shame, sitting on the sofa, the tears running down his cheeks.
>
> And Clarissa had leant forward, taken his hand, drawn him to her, kissed him—actually had felt his face on hers before she could down the brandishing of silver-flashing plumes like pampas grass in a tropic gale in her breast, which, subsiding, left her holding his hand, patting his knee, and feeling as she sat back extraordinarily at her ease with him and light-hearted, all in a clap it came over her, If I had married him, this gaiety would have been mine all day!

Her "irrepressible irritation" has issued in other irrepressible feelings. But Peter, knowing nothing of those feelings, thinks she is merely humoring him, that their battle has not been resolved.

Anyone who reads Virginia Woolf's diary can guess that Clarissa, in her emotional complexities, is a partial self-portrait and that the novel contains a double portrait of Leonard Woolf in two different aspects of himself: the protective, self-denying Richard Dalloway, expert in matters of government and politics, insistent on his wife's hour of complete rest every afternoon, and the frustrated, passionate Peter Walsh, experienced in colonial administration, remembering his erotic history in the colonies. Leonard Woolf, while working as a respected colonial official in Ceylon, paid for weekly sex with a local prostitute. Returned to England, and married to Virginia Stephen, he was active in socialist politics, his skill and eloquence in constant demand.* *Mrs. Dalloway* is, in addition to its many public meanings, an extended private love letter addressed by a wife to her husband.

THE RELIGIOUS FEELING

Clarissa has had other moments of surprise at her own feelings toward someone who has no inkling that she feels anything at all. This happens to her, sometimes, when talking with a woman friend who might be "confessing . . . some scrape, some folly," and something emotionally intense occurs invisibly within herself. Clarissa thinks of such a moment while withdrawing to her

---

* Another novel with a double portrait of the author's husband is *Frankenstein*. Henry Clerval is the warm, generous Percy Bysshe Shelley who had courted the young Mary Godwin; Victor Frankenstein is the destructive, egoistic Percy Bysshe Shelley to whom Mary Shelley was now married. Possibly many other novels contain double portraits that remain unrecognized because the author's spouse, unlike Percy Shelley or Leonard Woolf, was never the subject of a biography.

lonely attic room early in the day. The book evokes it in the language of a sexual act, and Clarissa's memory of it is vivid and exact in portraying both the emotions of the act and its physical events:

> And whether it was pity, or their beauty, or that she was older, or some accident . . . she did undoubtedly then feel what men felt. Only for a moment; but it was enough. It was a sudden revelation, a tinge like a blush which one tried to check and then, as it spread, one yielded to its expansion, and rushed to the farthest verge and there quivered and felt the world come closer, swollen with some astonishing significance, some pressure of rapture, which split its thin skin and gushed and poured with an extraordinary alleviation over the cracks and sores. Then, for that moment, she had seen an illumination; a match burning in a crocus; an inner meaning almost expressed. But the close withdrew; the hard softened. It was over—the moment.

One of the many striking things about this moment is that it is impossible to disentangle the male and female elements in it—and although "the moment" occurs while Clarissa is talking with a woman, in the very next sentence, it seems instead to have occurred with a man: that next sentence begins "Against such moments (with women too)," as if this moment had not occurred with a woman. And all this takes place during what seems from the outside a perfectly ordinary conversation about a younger woman's scrape or folly.*

---

* Virginia Woolf seems deliberately to have written about sex in a manner different from Joyce's. "Mr. Joyce's indecency in *Ulysses*," she wrote in "Mr. Bennett and Mrs. Brown," "seems to me the conscious and calculated indecency of a desperate man who feels that in order to breathe he must

And Clarissa's thoughts about that moment now remind her of Sally Seton, who kissed her on the lips when Sally was staying at Bourton after escaping from her family home after a fight with her parents. Sally has now become an effusive, conventional matron, proud of her rich self-made husband, proclaiming "I have five enormous boys." Thirty-three years ago Sally impressed Clarissa by running down the hall naked, shocking the housekeeper; she picked "all sorts of flowers that had never been seen together—cut their heads off, and made them swim on the top of water in bowls." Her "effect was extraordinary": in the language of recent film criticism, she was Clarissa's manic pixie dream girl who, delighting in dramatic gestures, once picked up a flower and kissed Clarissa on the lips, leaving Clarissa with a startled sense of "the revelation, the religious feeling!"*

So, today, Clarissa wonders, "This question of love (she thought, putting her coat away), this falling in love with women. Take Sally Seton; her relation in the old days with Sally Seton. Had not that, after all, been love?"

She has already been thinking about her eighteen-year-old daughter Elizabeth's feelings for the odious Miss Kilman. Now she remembers her own feelings when she was Elizabeth's age and exclaimed aloud about Sally, "She is beneath this roof!"

But this is only a memory. The old feelings are gone. "No [she continues], the words meant absolutely nothing to her now. She could not even get an echo of her old emotion"—and then,

---

    break the windows. At moments, when the window is broken, he is magnificent. But what a waste of energy!"

  * Virginia Woolf had a sharp eye for the erotic naïveté of the self-dramatizing wild child who ran down the hall naked. At the end of the book, Peter tells Sally that his first wife was "a perfect goose" but "we had a splendid time of it." Sally has no idea what he is talking about: "How could that be? Sally wondered; what did he mean?"

for a brief moment, as she remembers it, "the old feeling began to come back to her." But then it dissolves, and Clarissa again withdraws into the chill at her center, where "something central which permeated" ought to have been: "she had a sudden spasm, as if, while she mused, the icy claws had had the chance to fix in her."

THE PURITY, THE INTEGRITY

Lively discussions of *Mrs. Dalloway* often grind to a halt over the question of which sexual label ought to be assigned to Clarissa. But Virginia Woolf herself had strong moral and intellectual reasons for refusing to use any such labels.

In the same way that Virginia Woolf did not want to be "this or that," did not "want to be anything when I'm writing," Clarissa's great merit—which seems to make possible her triumph near the end of the book—is that she doesn't want to "be anything" and doesn't want anyone else to "be anything." This merit is inseparable from her faults. She evades other people; she refuses intimacy; but she doesn't try to impose categories on them. Much of the paragraph near the start of the book where she would not say of Peter or herself, "I am this, I am that," is about the way in which she is not this and not that—not anything categorizable by a noun or adjective. "She felt very young; at the same time unspeakably aged. She sliced like a knife through everything; at the same time was outside, looking on." The "life within" is never *this* or *that*: it has no age, no ethnicity, no skin color. It also has no gender: its proper pronoun is the first person singular. Auden wrote that in all languages (or in all that he knew about) the first-person and second-person pronouns *I* and *you* have no grammatical gender; only third-person pronouns assign a gender category to someone over there who isn't being spoken *to* or *with* face to face.*

Virginia Woolf never assigns a category to Clarissa's feelings for Sally or for Peter. The question that interests both Clarissa and her author is, in Clarissa's words, "was that love?," not what kind of love it was. Virginia Woolf recognizes a distinction that tends to get obscured in the current culture's ideas about collective identity: the difference between, on the one hand, what other people label you as being (as *this* or as *that*) and, on the other hand, what you actually are or want to be. Virginia Woolf wrote of "real people . . . of an unreal type." Real people are killed because someone takes them as being of an unreal type. There is no such thing as witchcraft and no such thing as a witch, but you can be killed for being one.† To see individuals as types—to objectify them as instances of "an unreal type"—is to efface their personhood; and to deny individual persons their dignity, their freedom, their right to justice, because you perceive them as members of a type, or as outsiders to your own unreal type, is murderously unjust.

A wonderfully clarifying moment occurs early in Virginia Woolf's fantasy novel *Orlando* (1928), in which Orlando (who at the end of the book is still alive after three hundred years, never having noticed anything strange about this) falls into a deep sleep for seven days and, on waking, discovers that he has become a

---

* Strikingly few counterexamples of gender-specific first or second person pronouns seem to exist; linguists report that they occur in Thai, Hebrew, archaic Japanese, and only a few others among seven thousand living languages and hundreds of recorded dead ones.

† This is an inadequate reflection of a more complex argument in Barbara J. Fields's 1990 essay "Slavery, Race and Ideology in the United States of America," reprinted in her book (with Karen Fields), *Racecraft: The Soul of Inequality in American Life* (2022).

woman. (As far as Virginia Woolf knew at the time, this was nothing more than a fantasy; it never occurred to her that something like it might happen in reality.) The narrator reflects on this transformation: "Orlando had become a woman—there is no denying it. But in every other respect, Orlando remained precisely as he had been. The change of sex, though it altered their future, did nothing whatever to alter their identity."

Orlando's future has changed along with her sex; she will have different bodily experiences; she will be subject to different expectations; she will perceive herself, and others will perceive her, as an instance of a "type." But she remains Orlando herself, her identity unaltered, because, for Virginia Woolf, "identity" is unique to one person, not something shared or collective.

Erich Auerbach, some of whose praise for Virginia Woolf I quoted earlier, wrote that she had discovered in her fiction:

> something new and elemental . . . nothing less than the wealth of reality and depth of life in every moment to which we surrender ourselves without prejudice. To be sure, what happens in that moment . . . concerns in a very personal way the individuals who live in it, but it also (and for that very reason) concerns the elementary things which [people]* in general have in common.

The more those moments are explored, Auerbach continued, "the more the elementary things which our lives have in common come to light." Auerbach found the special quality of Virginia Woolf's genius in her sense that the only way to understand all

---

* Auerbach wrote "*die Menschen*," i.e., "people," which the English translator Willard R. Trask in 1953, following the convention of the time, rendered as "men," meaning "people, human beings."

human beings is through the "difficult business of intimacy" with one.

Because she refuses to think of herself or Sally or Peter as this or as that, Clarissa's feelings about them have a lot to do with "the elementary things which [people] in general have in common," and with what all varieties of love have in common. About her feelings for Sally, about what she thinks of as "the revelation, the religious feeling," she now asks herself, "What was this except being in love?" And she goes on to think about what the specific qualities of that love were, and what were the common, generalizable conditions in which that love could emerge: "The strange thing, on looking back, was the purity, the integrity, of her feeling for Sally. It was not like one's feeling for a man. It was completely disinterested, and besides, it had a quality which could only exist between women, between women just grown up."

"It was completely disinterested"—meaning that her love wanted nothing from Sally (*disinterested* does not mean *uninterested*), unlike "one's feeling for a man," which always wants something from him. Love, as Clarissa thinks about it in these sentences, does not *want* anything. She remembers "doing her hair in a kind of ecstasy" because Sally was under the same roof; and Clarissa's love for Sally was precisely that disinterested ecstasy, a love that asked nothing more of Sally than that she be there and that she be herself.

Clarissa's feelings about love, and about everything else, keep changing as circumstances change. Later in the book, when she thinks about Elizabeth possibly in love with Miss Kilman, Clarissa no longer thinks of love as something pure, disinterested, and driven by ecstasy, as she herself thought at Elizabeth's age, but as something domineering, jealous, and cruel, driven by lust for power. Both her views are right; each responds to a different aspect or effect of love, although the book leaves no doubt about which aspect it imagines as more conducive to happiness.

When Clarissa says that her disinterested love for Sally was not like her self-interested feelings for a man, she is mostly right about herself, but she doesn't realize something that the book recognizes: that, for herself as for others, love that includes sexual desire can nonetheless be disinterested, exactly as her love for Sally was disinterested. She assumes that love between the sexes includes desire, and therefore can't have what she calls "the purity, the integrity," of her feelings for Sally. But in fact Peter Walsh's love for Clarissa, however much it was driven by desire in the past, has now become a love that has all the integrity and disinterestedness of Clarissa's old love for Sally. Peter's love urgently desires something, but there is nothing possessive about that desire.

Auden once remarked that what love desires is the self-actualization of the beloved. The lover doesn't want to possess—doesn't want to make an object of—the beloved; the lover wants the beloved to become the beloved's self. (One of Auden's poems says of the ego, "The aim of its eros is to create a soul."*) What Peter wants is for Clarissa to become "Clarissa herself," not the perfect hostess, not Mrs. Richard Dalloway. When he heard the bells strike the hour and thought of "Clarissa herself," he wondered a moment later "why had he been so profoundly happy

---

* Auden said in a lecture (reconstructed from a listener's notes) on Shakespeare's sonnets: "Falling in love is an intense interest in the existence of another person. That existence is not alone an object of knowledge; nor is it exclusively a goal of desire." That "intense interest" also applies to oneself: "Falling in love is the discovery of what 'I exist' means." And: "Because you exist, my existence becomes important" (*Lectures on Shakespeare*, ed. Arthur Kirsch, 2000, 88–89).

when the clock was striking"—not knowing that he was happy because he was remembering Clarissa herself. He has no erotic desire for her; he has deflected that desire to Daisy in India who promises to give him everything he wants. He is frustrated by Clarissa, but not because he can't have her. He is frustrated because, wanting her to be herself, he knows that she keeps thinking of herself—as she does at the start of the book—as "this being Mrs. Dalloway; not even Clarissa any more; this being Mrs. Richard Dalloway."*

And in the heartbreaking moment when Septimus Warren Smith briefly emerges from his madness minutes before his suicide, and talks lucidly with his wife, Lucrezia has this grateful thought: "He had become himself then."

When Clarissa tells herself that desire is possessive, that it is not disinterested, she is denying, as she often does, her own experience. In those moments of ordinary-seeming talk with another woman, when she felt "the world come closer, swollen with some astonishing significance, some pressure of rapture" that "gushed and poured"—before "the close withdrew, the hard softened"—in those moments when "she did undoubtedly then feel what men felt," she experienced something that was both erotic and unpossessive, exactly what Auden described as one of the great varieties of visionary experience, "the Vision of Eros," in which erotic desire is transfigured into an ecstatic sense of reverence, gratitude, and awe.

---

* On its last page, the book makes a point about the different names that identify different selves in the same person, the personal name that speaks personally, the shared family name that speaks conventionally: "'Richard has improved. You are right,' said Sally. . . . 'What does the brain matter,' said Lady Rosseter [Sally's title], getting up, 'compared with the heart?'" Zadie Smith, Virginia Woolf's direct literary heir, uses the same technique on the last page of her novel *NW* (2012), where the same person acts under both of the two names that she uses for herself: "Natalie dialed it [a phone number]. It was Keisha who did the talking."

What Clarissa's visionary moment points toward, among many other things, is that a sexual act, in the emotionally intimate context of intense personal love, can share in the integrity and purity that Clarissa remembers in her feelings for Sally. In this kind of sexuality, whatever else may be happening, whatever secret rituals of power, objectification, and magical substitution may also be involved, a sexual act is a form of mutual attention and mutual self-realization. This is what the Anglican wedding ceremony has in mind in the vow that follows "With this ring I thee wed," the vow that says: "With my body I thee worship."

Peter Walsh is frustrated because he has been focusing his attention on Clarissa as a person, someone with whom another person could be emotionally intimate, while Clarissa wants to be visible in her social role as hostess but invisible to anyone's personal attention. She rejects that attention as possessive and domineering, an invasion of the self, a violation of the soul's privacy. What finally breaks through her evasions is not someone else's attention but someone else's death, the death of Septimus Warren Smith, the death that makes her cry out inwardly, "Oh . . . in the middle of my party, here's death," the death that provokes her to feel what Septimus felt, the "rusty spikes, . . . the suffocation of blackness."

"But why had he done it?" she asks, and guesses that he had done it in order to preserve the integrity of the self that she has spent her life corrupting: "A thing there was that mattered; a thing, wreathed about with chatter, defaced, obscured in her own life, let drop every day in corruption, lies, chatter. This he had preserved."*

---

* "This he had preserved" was a last-minute addition, marked by Virginia Woolf in the proofs of the British edition.

And in the little room away from her party, Clarissa sees the value of the thing that mattered within herself, the thing that mattered that *is* herself. She sees this—in the words that the book used earlier when a sudden erotic vision gave her a sense of another person's value—"Only for a moment; but it was enough."

And as she sees this value in herself, she experiences Septimus's death as a means by which, without his knowing it, he has communicated with her: "Death was an attempt to communicate"—not mere death, but a death chosen as a means of communication: "people feeling the impossibility of reaching the centre which, mystically, evaded them; closeness drew apart; rapture faded; one was alone. There was an embrace in death."

Earlier, Clarissa thought she lacked "something central which permeated." Now she sees this, not as something she lacks, but as something barred from everyone by "the impossibility of reaching" it, although an embrace, even an embrace in death, can overcome that impossibility and guide her there. She experiences Septimus's death as an act of attention to herself, to the center which has evaded her until someone else attends to it—unlike her gentle, decent husband who is content to leave its privacy undisturbed. Septimus, as he flung himself from the window, cried, "I'll give it you!"* evidently thinking of the doctor coming through the door, but it is Clarissa who accepts his gift.

A person is someone who can say both *I* and *you* (the singular *you*, or *thou*) in a way that means something. What this magnificent passage dramatizes is that any realization of the value of oneself is simultaneously "an attempt to communicate" with

---

* Virginia Woolf followed older standard English usage by omitting "to" between "give" and "you," where American readers would expect it. In *Jacob's Room* (1922) Betty Flanders wonders "who could give it her" (miscorrected by the Penguin Classics editor to "give it to her").

another self. An *I* becomes itself as it seeks a *thou* to connect with—which is one reason why love of oneself is said to be a necessary condition of love for one's neighbor.

After a few more moments in the little room, Clarissa parts the curtains, and, "Oh, but how surprising!—in the room opposite the old lady stared straight at her!" This is the same old lady whom Clarissa had observed from her window a few hours earlier. Now Clarissa is the one being stared at—or, at least, she feels herself being stared at, she feels herself the subject of someone else's attention. She cannot tell whether the old lady actually sees her, but just as Septimus, through his death, provoked her to find the secret center of herself, now the old lady provokes her to see herself in relation to another living self, not only as *I*, Clarissa, but also as *thou*, the person whom the old lady is staring at. And now, for the first time in the book, having seen the thing that matters within her, she goes off to find the other selves who matter *to* her. This is what she thinks: "But she must go back. She must assemble. She must find Sally and Peter. And she came in from the little room."

The second of these sentences is a compressed work of poetic genius, and may include the only instance in English of the verb "to assemble" used intransitively about a single person, not about a group of persons or things. In three words, the sentence makes the connection between the self and love that the rest of the book has been making from the start. In its position following the first sentence, "But she must go back," this second sentence means that Clarissa must pull herself together and take actions. In its position preceding the third sentence, "She must find Sally and Peter," it means that she must assemble, not with the laughing crowd at her party, but with the two selves whom she has loved. She has found an answer, inexpressible in words, to "this question of love."

EPILOGUE

The Afterlife of the Text

> *The difficulty about criticism is that it is so superficial. The writer has gone so much deeper. . . . Our criticism is only a birds eye view of the pinnacle of an iceberg. The rest under water.*
> —The Diary of Virginia Woolf, 16 August 1933

Scholarship about the great epics began in Athens, with textual commentaries (*scholia*) on Homer. While *Mrs. Dalloway* was still in copyright, critics could write about it in books and essays, but no one could publish an annotated edition, nor any version of the text that deviated from that issued by its original publishers, the Hogarth Press in Britain and Harcourt, Brace in the United States. During that period, only one edited and partly annotated text appeared, as one of ten volumes in a "Definitive Collected Edition of the Novels of Virginia Woolf," published by the Hogarth Press in 1990 in an obvious effort to corner the market before the copyright on her works expired in Britain on 1 January 1992.

The term of copyright in Britain was then fifty years following an author's death, extending to the end of the fiftieth calendar year; Virginia Woolf had died in 1941. A few years after the copyright expired in 1992, a change in British law extended the term to seventy years, so Virginia Woolf's work returned to copyright from 1996 through 2011. In the United States, the copyright on *Mrs. Dalloway* expired on 1 January 2016, at the end of the calendar year ninety years following its first American publication.

In Britain, the novel was published on 14 May 1925 (the same day as the American edition) by Leonard and Virginia Woolf's Hogarth Press, which had hired out the printing to the firm of R. & R. Clark, Edinburgh.* The printers provided at least three sets of page proofs, and Virginia Woolf made three separate sets of corrections, apparently sending off the first before she corrected the second, and sending off the second before she corrected the third. Having corrected the first set, she bound it by hand and sent it to her friend Jacques Raverat so that it could be read to him before he died. She then corrected the second set and sent it off to America, where a compositor retyped the text for the edition published by Harcourt, Brace. She then corrected the third set and sent it off to Edinburgh so that the printers could incorporate her corrections and changes for the Hogarth Press edition.† As a result of this sequence of changes, each

---

* The visual design of the book, specified in a letter from Leonard Woolf to the printers, may have originated with Virginia Woolf, who was by this time an expert printer. The design called for a book in Crown Octavo size, set in 12-point Caslon Old Style, with twenty-eight lines to a page, and a page header with the title and page number between thin horizontal rules.

† Virginia Woolf wrote in her diary on 6 January 1925 that her revised text, having been read by Leonard Woolf, "is sent off to Clarks [in Edinburgh], and proofs will come next week. This is for Harcourt Brace..." "This" seems to refer to proofs intended for the Harcourt edition, not for the Hogarth edition; the proofs sent to Harcourt (now in the Lilly Library at Indiana University) have dates 13 through 19 January 1925 stamped by the printer, and are stamped "First Proof." There may or may not have been a second proof; if so, it is lost.

apparently made independently, the American and British editions differ in subtly crucial ways in tone and content, and the book familiar to American readers is softer and less disturbing than the one familiar to British readers.

More than a dozen annotated editions have appeared since the copyright expired. Those published in Britain, with one exception, have followed the British text; those published in the United States, with one partial exception, have followed the American text. A 1996 British edition from the Shakespeare Head Press was edited by an American who made an incoherent argument for his decision to base its text on the proofs of the 1925 American edition, not on the later British text. A 2021 American edition from Liveright, *The Annotated Mrs. Dalloway*, used the British text but inserted a sentence from the American text that Virginia Woolf, when preparing the British text, had dropped at the last minute.*

With one exception, the editions that I use and admire are based, with minor variations, on the British text. G. Patton Wright's 1990 edition for the Hogarth Press's elegantly printed "Definitive Collected" series has an easily navigable set of textual notes, but invents needless changes to the text designed to smooth out minor inconsistencies in Peter Walsh's age and the color of Elizabeth's party dress. The 1992 Penguin Classics edition has a carefully considered text, with corrections and emendations by Stella McNichol, and an introduction by Elaine Showalter that remains, I think, the best single essay on the book.† The 2000 Oxford World's Classics edition by David

---

* The Liveright edition, on page 28, accidentally omits a long paragraph that begins "Everything had come to a standstill," following two brief paragraphs introducing Septimus.
† No one, it seems, pays much attention to the textual notes on which editors have expended their expertise and labor. The notes in Stella McNichol's

Bradshaw has a crisply informative introduction and notes, but its text is based not on the first British edition, but on a later, reset edition published by the Hogarth Press in 1942, a year after the author's death, with minor changes to spelling, punctuation, and layout introduced by the printer. The edition best suited to scholars and obsessive readers is Anne Fernald's 2015 volume in the Cambridge Edition of the Works of Virginia Woolf, based closely on the 1925 text with extensive, well-focused notes and an almost complete record of textual variants in the marked proofs and all the printed editions worth noticing. The best edition based on the American text, and the most useful edition for anyone interested in the intellectual and historical background, is Anne Fernald's 2021 Norton Critical Edition, which includes, among much ancillary material ranging from Homer to W. H. R. Rivers, Virginia Woolf's diary entries and letters about the book, but suffers from the rebarbative typography that Norton uses for all its Critical Editions.

The eyes of many intelligent readers glaze over when faced with even a paragraph about textual minutiae. But Anne Fernald's long account, in her Cambridge edition, of Virginia Woolf's manuscripts, typescripts, and proofs—each the product of, in J. Alfred Prufrock's phrase, "a hundred visions and revisions, / Before the taking of a toast and tea"—has the excitement

---

1992 Penguin Classics edition have been reprinted more than thirty times, apparently without anyone having noticed that an editorial or printing error left one lengthy note without any indication of the passage in the text that it refers to. (In the 1992 British edition the note is on page 231, in the 2021 American edition page 178; both editions fail to explain that the note refers to the paragraph on British page 144, American page 111, that begins "But said Miss Kilman," where McNichol rejects an emendation made by G. Patton Wright in his 1990 edition.) Inevitably, errors and omissions also occur in every other edition that includes a list of textual variants.

of a detective novel. My next few paragraphs touch on only a few of the story's complications and surprises.*

The most striking difference between the British and American texts occurs near the end of the book, when Clarissa is about to return to her party from the little room, after having experienced Septimus's death, having confronted her own failure to preserve the "thing there was that mattered," and having recognized "her disaster—her disgrace," her wish for success, "Lady Bexborough and the rest of it." Clarissa's experience in the little room has been purgatorial, and she now emerges from purgatory: she sees in the solitude of the old lady opposite staring straight at her none of the inner suffering that, until this moment, has tormented her own solitude: "It was fascinating, with people still laughing and shouting in the drawing-room, to watch that old woman, quite quietly, going to bed alone."

She remembers Septimus, but "she did not pity him, with all this going on." To pity someone, in Virginia Woolf's vocabulary, is to disdain them as lesser than oneself; but Septimus is Clarissa's double, and she pities neither him nor herself. Then the old lady puts out her light, and "the whole house was dark now with this going on." Clarissa keeps repeating varieties of the phrase "with this going on," the point being that she has, for the moment at least, escaped from the social world of parties, power,

---

* A few editors have noticed that the British text has Clarissa thinking, about love and religion, "How destestable, how destestable they are!" with an intrusive "s" in the first instance. Did Virginia Woolf use this uncommon variant in her typescript? (Dickens used it in *Bleak House*, Forster in *Howards End*, Lawrence in the American edition of *Aaron's Rod*, although subsequent editions of all these books tend to regularize it.) Did she use it once, as in the printed text, or twice, the second instance having been corrected by a compositor? An editor loses sleep over these questions.

and status that she had relied on for her whole being, and can find her own way, "with all this going on."

"But what an extraordinary night," she thinks, and the American, earlier, version of the text continues:

> She felt somehow very like him—the young man who had killed himself. She felt glad that he had done it; thrown it away. The clock was striking. The leaden circles dissolved in the air. He made her feel the beauty; made her feel the fun. But she must go back. She must assemble. She must find Sally and Peter. And she came in from the little room.

Virginia Woolf's final version in the British text differs in two ways. After the phrase "thrown it away," the British text has "while they went on living." And the British version omits the sentence "He made her feel the beauty; made her feel the fun."

Like every writer, Virginia Woolf discovered what she wanted to say in the act of writing: "I begin to see what I had in my mind," she wrote when revising *The Waves*. When she began *Mrs. Dalloway* she wrote in her diary, "I want to give life and death, sanity and insanity." The effect of her final revision to the British text is to emphasize, in a way that she had not done before, that what is at stake, in this episode and in the novel as a whole, is not beauty and fun, but life and death. The sentence about beauty and fun tempts readers into trivializing the book, and Virginia Woolf knew exactly what she was doing when she removed that temptation. The phrase "while they went on living," added in the British text, absent from the American, makes the same point about what is at stake.

Other revisions, earlier in the book, make similar points. For example, Peter remembers the young Clarissa's appalled reaction when told that a neighbor had married the housemaid with whom he had had a child, and, in the American text, thinks: "it was her manner that annoyed him; timid; hard, something arrogant; unimaginative; prudish." The British text lacks "something" and "unimaginative," and the effect of removing "unimaginative" is to emphasize that what annoys Peter is not Clarissa's imagination but her hardness and prudery. Her imagination exists in the same amoral realm with the beauty and fun that Virginia Woolf omitted later in the book. Another last-minute revision, also in the episode set in the little room, removes a distracting glance at Richard that blurred the focus on Clarissa herself. The earlier, American text has a paragraph that begins, "It was due to Richard; she had never been so happy." The final British text replaces this with, "Odd, incredible; she had never been so happy." The revised phrase points to Clarissa's uncanny experience of Septimus, and away from the underlying security provided by Richard.

British readers, or at least those who are not academic specialists, have never seen the sentence in which Clarissa feels the beauty and the fun, and British editors seem never to mention it. Only American readers, who learned to love the book in its American version, seem to favor the sentence, so much so that some perceive it as the moral of the book. In her Cambridge edition, Anne Fernald writes that "a case can be made for preferring" the American reading, although she does no more than argue the case in her introduction, leaving the British text unchanged, as the policy of the Cambridge edition requires.* The American editor of *The Annotated Mrs. Dalloway*, Merve

---

* Fernald suggests that Virginia Woolf may have omitted the sentence in order to leave room for a section break at the end of the paragraph. This seems unlikely; had she wanted to retain the sentence *and* leave room for a section break, she could easily have done so by cutting two words from a chatty paragraph elsewhere on the page.

Emre, having inserted the American-edition sentence into the British text, produced a hybrid paragraph that retains the British-edition phrase "while they went on living." Virginia Woolf thought in paragraphs as well as in sentences, and this hybrid is a paragraph that the author never wrote or imagined.*

Having second-guessed Virginia Woolf's revision, Merve Emre claimed to have been obligated to decide whether to accept or reject it: "Any editor must choose whether to include the line ... or to omit it entirely." No other editor has made that choice; none has felt free to make it. Editions based on the American text include the sentence; editions based on the British text do not. The degree to which an editor is free to shape a text depends entirely on the kinds of sources that the editor must work with. An editor of Virginia Woolf—who made her own typescripts and corrected her own proofs, and was joint owner with her husband of her own publishing firm—has different freedoms and different responsibilities from those of an editor of almost any other writer.

Editors of ancient manuscripts and early printed books are obliged to work from manuscripts and published texts that their authors never supervised and may never have seen. *King Lear* is a well-known extreme case that exemplifies a common problem. An editor of the play must work from two very different texts: the First Quarto, published without Shakespeare's authorization, and the First Folio, published after his death. No one knows how close either text is to anything that Shakespeare

---

* Among American editors and critics, G. Patton Wright may be unique in preferring the British text. He wrote in his 1990 Hogarth Press edition: "This deletion can be justified on grounds of preserving consistency of tone, for given the serious nature of Clarissa's internal monologue in the room apart, it is gratuitous to have her think that Septimus Smith's suicide 'made her feel the fun.'"

himself wrote; no one knows if any of the differences between the two texts represent his revisions; so a plausible case can be made for combining—as almost all editors have done—the Quarto and Folio into a single "eclectic" text, with each editor making different choices between conflicting passages in the two versions.

The two published texts of *Mrs. Dalloway* present a far more limited set of choices. Each text has its own integrity: the American text represents one stage of Virginia Woolf's revisions; the British text represents a later one. Editors can argue over the merits of her changes, but the one categorical imperative of textual editing is this: in the absence of some overwhelming and self-evident reason to do otherwise, you must not favor your opinion over an author's judgment. Virginia Woolf's judgment produced these spare and morally focused sentences in the British text: "She felt glad that he had done it; thrown it away while they went on living. The clock was striking. The leaden circles dissolved in the air. But she must go back. She must assemble. She must find Sally and Peter. And she came in from the little room."

THE FACTS OF THE MATTER

Virginia Woolf, like most writers, lost interest in her books soon after they were published. She wrote in her 1928 introduction to an American Modern Library reissue of *Mrs. Dalloway*:

> And the author's mind . . . is as inhospitable to its offspring as the hen sparrow is to hers. Once the young birds can fly, fly they must; and by the time they have fluttered out of the nest the mother bird has begun to think perhaps of another brood. In the

same way once a book is printed and published it ceases to be the property of the author; he commits it to the care of other people; all his attention is claimed by some new book . . .

Soon after the first British edition of *Mrs. Dalloway* was printed in May 1925, Virginia Woolf made two changes to the text, both in the same paragraph, for a second printing in September. In 1929, a year after she had written that *Mrs. Dalloway* had fluttered out of the nest, she made seven more changes for a 1929 "Uniform Edition" of her novels, although possibly she had marked these changes earlier in her own copy of the book.

Of the two changes she made in 1925, the first was a factual correction of the name of the club where, as the mysterious official car moves through London, tall, robust men are standing in the bow window, ready to attend their Sovereign to the cannon's mouth. The first edition identified the club as Brooks's, a Whig, later a Liberal, club. But the famous bow window was on the ground floor of White's, the Tory club on the opposite side of St. James's Street. For the novel, White's was both architecturally and politically the more accurate choice, and Virginia Woolf was surely responsible for the change in the second printing.

The second change, a few lines later, seems less clearly motivated. As the car moves through the streets, in the first printing "syphons of soda water seemed to approve." In the second printing they became "bottles of soda water," making the image less vivid, but perhaps removing an alliteration of the kind that Virginia Woolf usually reserved for poetic passages, like the one in Peter's dream where "fishermen flounder through floods." The change to "bottles" survived into all later Hogarth Press printings, and thus into the Oxford World's Classics edition, although it is ignored in Stella McNichol's Penguin Classics edition and explicitly rejected in G. Patton Wright's Hogarth Press edition and in Anne E. Fernald's Cambridge edition. But a change to a printing plate was costly, and it is hard to imagine that anyone other than Virginia Woolf would have chosen to make it.*

Virginia Woolf seems to have made her seven changes in the 1929 "Uniform Edition" mostly for the sake of euphony and grammar, not content. For example, early in the 1925 text, Clarissa thinks about Peter Walsh, "Yet, after all, how much she owed to him later"; grammatically, however, the antecedent of "him" is her German tutor Joseph Breitkopf a few lines earlier. In 1929 the sentence reads "Yet how much she owed to Peter Walsh later." (The two words "after all" probably got dropped for typographic reasons, because Virginia Woolf knew they could not fit into the reset line.) In 1925, Clarissa cried to Peter as he left her house in the morning, "My party to-night! Remember my party to-night!" In 1929, the first "to-night" disappeared, apparently sacrificed for rhythm's sake.†

---

* Until I saw copies of both the first and second printings, I had hoped that the change had been inadvertent: I wanted to believe that a compositor at R. & R. Clark had reset the entire paragraph, inattentively mistyping "bottles" for "syphons" after having attentively changed "Brooks's" to "White's." But this seems impossible. All the other lines in the paragraph—which has "White's" on one page and "bottles" on the next—are typographically identical in both printings, and only two lines of type needed to be replaced in order to make the two changes. Occam's razor suggests that the author-publisher initiated both.

† The other five changes in 1929 were these: In Clarissa's erotic vision, an exclamation mark is replaced by a full stop after "alleviation over the cracks and sores." In his visit to Sir William Bradshaw, Septimus wonders in 1925 "Would they let him off then, Holmes Bradshaw?"; in 1929 the names are separated by a comma. In 1925, in the paragraph that begins "And of course she enjoyed life" Peter Walsh comes out of the park holding "his hat in hand"; in 1929 he holds "his hat in his hand" (no editor seems to have noticed this change). In 1925, in the paragraph that begins "'Evans!' he cried," in the final scene of Septimus's madness, "The screen, the coal-scuttle, the sideboard remained him"; in 1929 they "remained to him." As Peter makes his way to Clarissa's party he buys a newspaper with a copper coin, and this

For all readers, even the most scholarly, a printed text has an air of authority that makes anything in it that is not obviously a misprint seem inevitable and right. But almost every printed book is invisibly marred by the inattention and misjudgment of authors, typists, and compositors.

The least bad among possible editions, I think, would be one that reproduces the 1929 text, correcting a mistyped "commerical" to "commercial," and with at most four other changes.* The first would add a grammatically required comma following "it" in Peter's thought as he looks at Gordon's statue, "he, too, had made it, the great renunciation"; in the surviving proofs, where Virginia Woolf circled "too" and marked it to be moved before "had made it," the printer seems to have misinterpreted her markup by deleting the comma after "it." The second change would shift a misplaced "of" where Lady Bruton is said never to "read a word poetry of herself." A third would correct an obvious typing error near the end of the book that mistakenly has Richard, not Peter, saying of the Bradshaws "That they're damnable humbugs," in response to the question about them that "Sally whispered" while talking with Peter. The point of Peter saying this is that he can join Clarissa, Richard, and Lucrezia in their disdain for Sir William, and it is impossible that Richard could have said it: he is on the other side of the room, where he had been speaking with the Bradshaws, and could not have heard or answered Sally's whispered question to Peter.

The fourth, earlier in the party, would restore from the proofs Virginia Woolf's invented word "vagulous" in the phrase

---

action is reported within a parenthesis; in 1925 a second parenthesis inside the first says "(he had held out that copper millions of times)"; in 1929 the inner opening parenthesis becomes a semi-colon, the inner closing one becomes a dash.

* As I note in the preface to this book, such an edition is to be published by New York Review Books in 2025.

that in all British texts reads "that vagous phosphorescence, old Mrs. Hilbery." Virginia Woolf seems to have invented the word by translating a Latin diminutive in Hadrian's "Animula vagula blandula," his poem addressed to his wandering, charming little soul; the masculine form of *vagula* is *vagulus*.* "Vagulous" occurs in Virginia Woolf's early drafts of the novel, and in the proofs, and in the American edition. The word occurs twice in her diary; her invented verb "vagulate" occurs four times in her diary and letters, and "circumvagulation" once. The change in the British edition of the novel from "vagulous" to "vagous"—a word she never used anywhere—seems to have been made by a well-intentioned reader or compositor at R. & R. Clark, but "vagulous" is what she wrote, and "vagous" is a different word, not a correction. She admired Shakespeare's "word-coining power," feeling it "utterly outpace and outrace my own." T. S. Eliot invented "juvescence" for "Gerontion"; Virginia Woolf has the right to "vagulous."

W. H. Auden wrote in an elegy for W. B. Yeats, "The words of a dead man / Are modified in the guts of the living." He was thinking of the ways in which readers interpret a dead writer's work, but the words of a dead writer are also modified by the hands of the living when printed in new editions. When the Hogarth Press published a reset edition of *Mrs. Dalloway* in 1942 it tamed Virginia Woolf's wayward spelling and punctuation, so that, for example, "some one," in many but not all instances, became "someone."†

---

* At least two other early twentieth-century writers seem independently to have invented "vagulous," also by englishing Hadrian.

† Authors sometimes make errors in logic, but they are their own errors, and there is no way to guess whether they would have wanted a copyeditor to correct them before going into print. In the British edition, Lucrezia "would say" the English are so serious, "putting her arms round Septimus, her cheeks against his." The American edition corrected "cheeks" to the more

Anne Fernald, in her Cambridge edition, lists more than four hundred differences between the first British and the first American texts. Most are trivial variants in spelling or punctuation; around thirty involve one or more different words; a few, as in the sentence about beauty and fun, are decisive; some, like the division of the text into a different number of sections, are crucial to a reader's sense of the structure of the book. Virginia Woolf's first title for the book was *The Hours*—it was still her title seven months before publication—and the twelve sections into which she divided the text of the first British edition are a visible echo of her original intention. She seems to have settled on the twelve-part design at a late stage of revision, adding six section breaks while correcting proofs, and doing so only after she had removed the more direct indications of the hours that she had written into her earlier drafts. While Clarissa is alone in the little room, for example, she hears the clock striking, but the printed text does not specify, as her earlier drafts had specified, that it is striking "twelve times."*

This design is visible only in the first British edition of May 1925 and its three later printings in September 1925, September 1929, and February 1933. All other printings on both sides of the Atlantic—other than a very few scholarly texts starting in 1990—omit one or more of the section breaks and, by doing so, obscure the shape that Virginia Woolf chose for the book.

---

    plausible "cheek," as do some later editors. But Virginia Woolf may have intended the double plural "arms . . . cheeks."

* The early drafts are printed in *Virginia Woolf "The Hours": The British Museum Manuscript of* Mrs. Dalloway, transcribed and edited by Helen M. Wussow (2010); "strike twelve times" is on page 397. A facsimile edition of the drafts, with unnumbered pages, was published as *Virginia Woolf, Mrs. Dalloway, The Hours* (2019) by SP Books—Éditions de Saints Pères; it omits some additional material transcribed in Helen Wussow's edition from notebooks in The New York Public Library.

In the first British edition, the twelve sections are separated by one or two blank lines. In the first American edition, two of those blank-line breaks occur at the foot of a page and are therefore invisible; the printer neglected to add an asterisk or other typographic device that could indicate a break. Two additional breaks do not occur in the American text because Virginia Woolf inserted them in the British text only after sending off the American proofs. American readers, if they counted the sections, would have found eight, British readers twelve. Almost all later editions of the American text present the same eight sections. The posthumous, reset British edition first printed in 1942 lost one of the twelve breaks by omitting one of the two original blank lines after the third instance of the old woman's incomprehensible song, "ee um fah um so / foo swee too eem oo." After the fourth British printing in 1933, the only editions that break the text correctly into twelve sections seem to be G. Patton Wright's for the Hogarth Press, Anne Fernald's Cambridge edition, and Merve Emre's *Annotated Mrs. Dalloway*. The one serious fault in Stella McNichol's admirable Penguin Classics text is that it fails to restore the section break lost in 1942.

THE CRITIC TAKES COMMAND

Notes and introductions inevitably shade and shape the text that they offer to explain. Some editors' notes make it possible to perceive meanings in a text that would otherwise be obscured by the passage of time, like the "Indian women" whom Clarissa rails against. For readers coming to the book today, editors would do well to specify that Virginia Woolf, born in 1882, seems never to have had any sexual connotation in mind when she used the word "queer"—as she does nineteen times in *Mrs. Dalloway*. She was using the vocabulary of her class and era. Auden, twenty-five years younger, always used the word in its sexual sense, either suggestively or explicitly.

One subtle way in which a scholarly edition can falsify a book is through the visual material—maps, drawings, photographs—that it adds to the typographic text. *The Annotated Mrs. Dalloway* includes hundreds of illustrations, among them three photographs of an expensively dressed Katherine ("Kitty") Maxse, who provided a distant model for Clarissa Dalloway. Kitty Maxse, born in 1867, was a family friend and frequent visitor during Virginia Woolf's childhood; she died in 1922 when she fell from the top of her stairs. Virginia Woolf recorded in her diary that she had "died, suddenly," a standard euphemism for suicide, although there seems to be no other evidence of this. Kitty Maxse was, Virginia Woolf wrote, "very charming—very humorous," but added: "Not that I ever felt at my ease with her." For Virginia Woolf, she was a charming society hostess, fifteen years older than herself, about whom she had mixed feelings. Clarissa Dalloway is both a society hostess and a moral and psychological quest-hero who, despite her author's mixed feelings, achieves a depth of understanding unmatched in modern literature.*

Virginia Woolf hoped for "a close and equal alliance between" writer and reader; every reader joins in that alliance by creating mental images of Clarissa, Peter, and the others, images that each reader is convinced are true, even if they are entirely

---

* Virginia Woolf wrote in her diary (18 June 1925) that she had almost given up writing the novel "because I found Clarissa in some way tinselly. Then I invented her memories. But I think some distaste for her persisted. Yet, again, that was true to my feeling for Kitty . . ." Her tinselly qualities survived in the sentence about beauty and fun that appeared in the American text and disappeared from the British one.

unlike the images created by anyone else. This private image-making is an essential part of the act of reading, and helps to explain why no impersonal theoretical account of a book can ever be adequate. A photograph of Kitty Maxse in her finery invites a reader to objectify Clarissa Dalloway in ways that private image-making refuses to do. The effect of such a photograph—and the effect of the images proffered by filmed and staged adaptations of the book—is that of a social director telling readers what their relation to the writer ought to be, instead of leaving them alone to create the close and equal alliance that Virginia Woolf hoped for.

When one of her friends, after reading *To the Lighthouse*, complained that the meaning of the lighthouse itself had escaped him, she answered: "I meant *nothing* by The Lighthouse . . . [I] trusted that people would make it the deposit for their own emotions . . . I can't manage Symbolism except in this vague, generalised way. Whether it's right or wrong I don't know, but directly I'm told what a thing means, it becomes hateful to me."

In the same way that Clarissa is depersonalized by Peter when he dreams of her as a symbol—"the giant figure at the end of the ride," who will "let me blow to nothingness with the rest"—so she is depersonalized when a reader sees her image in a photograph of Kitty Maxse.

As symbolic meanings *generalize* a book, photographic images, and staged or filmed representations, *materialize* it. The action in *Mrs. Dalloway* is overwhelmingly the inward action that occurs when a character thinks or perceives. Virginia Woolf emphasizes this by briefly and occasionally glimpsing something from the outside or from someone else's perspective. Most of what the book has to say about Peter Walsh is a report of his words and thoughts, or of what Clarissa thinks about him. But when he rings Clarissa's doorbell early in the morning, the book sees him for a moment from the outside: "'Mrs. Dalloway will see me,' said the elderly man in the hall. 'Oh yes, she will see *me*,' he repeated, putting Lucy aside very benevolently, and running upstairs ever so quickly."

Then, for the next twenty pages, the book sees him from inside until the perspective shifts from Peter's inner life to Lucrezia's, and Peter becomes a visible object, "the man in grey"* whom Lucrezia sees through her tears, together with the nurse and the perambulator who had shared a bench with him as he dreamed. But this happens only for a moment, emphasizing that visual reality is not what the book cares about, compared with the fugal ebb and flow of thought that animates inner reality.

Mrs. Dalloway, like its model *Ulysses*, reproduces in miniature the wanderings of the parent and child heroes of the *Odyssey*, but the journeys in *Mrs. Dalloway* differ from those in both earlier books in one crucial way: while the travelers in all three books journey through the visible reality of geographical space, and while all the travelers do much invisible thinking on the way, Virginia Woolf's travelers tend to lose sight of their surroundings. James Joyce reportedly said of *Ulysses*, "I want to give a picture of Dublin so complete that if the city one day suddenly disappeared from the earth it could be reconstructed out of my book." *Mrs. Dalloway* takes a very different view of London. Its characters pursue their journeys through the inner geography of their minds, while their bodies move more or less automatically through unspecified physical space. Almost all the annotated modern editions of the book include one or more maps of London. In some editions, maps trace the characters' routes with dotted or colored lines, but in the three best-edited editions that

---

* "The man in grey" reappears six times in *Between the Acts*, where he is the gentleman farmer Haines secretly desired by Isa Oliver.

have maps—the editions made by Stella McNichol, David Bradshaw, and Anne Fernald in her Cambridge edition—the maps show landmarks only, not specific routes that someone took from one place to another. (Similarly, the map in Bonnie Kime Scott's 2005 annotated edition of the American text is marked with specific locations visited by the characters in the book, but does not pretend to trace their actual route.)*

The novel is psychologically accurate in its portrayal of its characters walking. They notice an occasional shop or landmark or street name, but they are not aware of the name of each street they walk on, and, for much of their travels, the novel doesn't bother to identify those streets. The maps that purport to trace their exact routes falsify the book by materializing those travels, by sending the characters arbitrarily down one street rather than another in the absence of any evidence in the text.

Furthermore, the geography of *Mrs. Dalloway* is subtly different from the geography of London itself. On her way from Westminster to Bond Street, Clarissa looks into the window of Hatchard's bookshop on Piccadilly, where she sees an open copy of *Cymbeline* and reads two solemn lines that she will repeat to herself later in the book. On the maps that purport to trace her exact route, Clarissa, in order to reach Hatchard's, exits Green Park and walks east on Piccadilly, passing Bond Street on her left, and continuing a few dozen yards to Hatchard's—and then she turns back to retrace her steps westward on Piccadilly until she reaches Bond Street and again turns north.† But nothing in

---

* Joyce also took pains to incorporate events that occurred on 6 June 1904. *Mrs. Dalloway* takes place on a Wednesday in June 1923, but, as David Bradshaw demonstrates in his Oxford World's Classics edition, the book makes it impossible to specify an exact date.

† Fernald's Norton Critical Edition, although not her Cambridge edition, has this kind of map, as does the Liveright *Annotated Mrs. Dalloway*, with exact

the book suggests that Clarissa reverses her direction after reaching Hatchard's, nor that she had any motive to walk eastward past Bond Street in order to look into Hatchard's window. This is confirmed by Virginia Woolf's skeletal sketch map of Clarissa's journey, reproduced in Anne Fernald's Cambridge edition, showing her route as three straight lines, one taking Clarissa northward through Green Park, the second eastward along Piccadilly, and the third northward up Bond Street, with no suggestion that she doubles back from Hatchard's. In the mental map of London that Virginia Woolf used when writing the novel, Hatchard's was not in its real physical location, but was located west of Bond Street, along Clarissa's direct route to the florist, where Clarissa could glance at it by chance.* The geography of the novel corresponds to Samuel Beckett's medicine in his novel *Watt*, where, as he explained in a footnote, "Haemophilia ... is an exclusively male disorder. But not in this work."†

Virginia Woolf portrayed the life within; scholars, by materializing her books, present the life without as the true, objective meaning of the life within. Something similar, but more extreme, occurs when a novelist or dramatist or filmmaker or choreographer or opera librettist makes an adaptation of the

---

routes printed in gorgeous colors. G. Patton Wright's edition has no map.

* This may have been a deliberate change from the more accurate geography of the 1923 story "Mrs. Dalloway in Bond Street," where Clarissa knowingly walks past Bond Street before turning back toward it: "There was St. James palace ... and now—she had passed Bond Street—she was by Hatchard's book shop."

† One minor geographical mystery in Virginia Woolf's novel *Jacob's Room* is the sentence on the first page, "Scarborough is seven hundred miles from Cornwall." The actual distance is around four hundred miles, but it is impossible to tell whether the error is in the mind of Jacob's mother Betty Flanders or the mind of the author.

book—typically presented as an homage to it—in a different medium or with a different story. *Mrs. Dalloway* has provoked many such adaptations and homages, perhaps more than any other novel of its century. These adaptations, although honored with prizes and admired by critics whose judgment I respect, may perhaps also confirm Auden's remark that "As readers, most of us, to some degree, are like those urchins who pencil mustaches on the faces of girls in advertisements." These adaptations seem to me unconscious acts of appropriation and diminishment, committed by writers and artists insensible to their resentment toward an artist vastly greater than themselves, and intent on reducing her unmanageable genius to some reassuringly categorizing and sentimental sense of life and art which she had the courage to refuse.

THE SHADOW OF DEATH

Clarissa's lonely purgatorial confrontation with death ends when she thinks, "But she must go back. She must assemble. She must find Sally and Peter. And she came in from the little room."

This ends the eleventh section of the book, and is followed by a break that Virginia Woolf marked in the proofs that she sent to Jacques Raverat; then neglected to mark in the American proof, resulting in its absence from the American edition; and then marked in her final proofs for the British edition.

The break is a crucial one. Following it, in the entire twelfth and last section, until almost the very end, Clarissa disappears. The section begins by emphasizing her absence: "'But where is Clarissa?' said Peter. He was sitting on the sofa with Sally.... 'Where's the woman gone to?' he asked. 'Where's Clarissa?'"

Sally and he both suppose "that there were people of importance . . . whom Clarissa had to be nice to, had to talk to. She was with them." But the book reports this explanation indirectly, rather than quoting it in the vivid way that it reports Peter's three questions asking where she is.

Beyond Sally and Peter's supposition, the book says nothing about where Clarissa is, nothing of what she is doing or thinking, not even whether anyone sees her in some other room. Peter and Sally are sitting on a sofa talking about her as the party gradually disintegrates around them. Elizabeth has joined her father Richard but is thinking about her poor dog howling. As Sir William and Lady Bradshaw make their way out, Sir William, who "was so interested in art," stops briefly to look at the engraver's name on a picture—possibly the same picture that had somehow provoked Clarissa to her sudden anger against Miss Kilman when she looked at its gilt frame earlier. "Even Ellie Henderson was going, nearly last of all." If anyone has seen or spoken to Clarissa, the book says nothing about it.

Peter and Sally, hoping to speak with Clarissa, remain on the sofa until, at last, Sally stands up to say goodbye to Richard. Peter says, "I will come," but he sits on for a moment. And he thinks:

> What is this terror? what is this ecstasy? he thought to himself.
> What is it that fills me with extraordinary excitement?
>   It is Clarissa, he said.
>   For there she was.

What has happened is not merely that Clarissa has stepped into the room; Peter Walsh is caught up in a vision of Clarissa herself, with all the terror and ecstasy of any sudden recognition of another self in its depth and fullness. He had already felt, a few hours earlier, the sound of the bells of St. Margaret's gliding into "the recesses of the heart . . . like Clarissa herself." Clarissa has already remembered that she and Peter always had the "power of communicating without words." And Peter remembers her "transcendental theory" that even after death, "the unseen part of us . . . might survive, be recovered somehow attached to this person or that."

The book has been shadowed from the start with thoughts of Clarissa's death. As the bells of St. Margaret's began ringing, Peter felt profoundly happy, but, then, a moment later:

> as the sound of St. Margaret's languished, he thought, She has been ill, and the sound expressed languor and suffering. It was her heart, he remembered; and the sudden loudness of the final stroke tolled for death that surprised in the midst of life, Clarissa falling where she stood, in her drawing-room. No! No! he cried. She is not dead! I am not old, he cried, and marched up Whitehall . . .

Virginia Woolf claimed that in her first plans for the book, Clarissa "was originally to kill herself, or perhaps merely die, at the end of her party." This original plan survives as a kind of shadow plot in the finished book, hinted at as a possibility, but not actual or real, as the threat of death that darkens all great comedies.* Clarissa is invisible in the final chapter, and Peter experiences her in the form of something that fills him "with extraordinary excitement," exactly as the unseen part of herself

---

* E. M. Forster may have been the one early reader to sense this shadow plot, although he got the details wrong. In "The Novels of Virginia Woolf" (*The New Criterion,* April 1926; reprinted in *Abinger Harvest,* 1936, as "The Early Novels of Virginia Woolf") he wrote of Clarissa: "Does she likewise commit suicide? I thought she did the first time I read the book . . ."

would have come to him had her transcendental theory been true, and had she now attached herself to "this person or that."

In fact Clarissa is not dead, as, to Peter's surprise, her Aunt "Helena Parry was not dead." But the story of Clarissa's death, and her recovery somehow attached to Peter, remains as a muted counterpoint to the actual story, in which Clarissa returns to her party inwardly transformed by her triumph in the little room. And she has communicated this to Peter without words. She has become herself—"Only for a moment; but it was enough."

For there she was. And still inspiring terror and ecstasy, still filling other selves with extraordinary excitement, there she remains.

ACKNOWLEDGMENTS

This book exists because the Columbia University Seminars asked me to give the Leonard Hasting Schoff Lectures in 2017, with the expectation that the lectures would, however belatedly, issue in a book published by Columbia University Press. I am grateful to Robert Pollack, Alice Newton, and the entire University Seminars Committee, and to Julie Crawford, Nicholas Dames, and Barbara J. Fields for their generous words of introduction when I delivered the lectures. I am grateful also to Philip Leventhal, who expertly shepherded the manuscript through the Press, and to the three anonymous readers who provided the Press with sharp-eyed, sympathetic readers' reports.

Hermione Lee is the critic and biographer from whom I have learned most about Virginia Woolf. Elaine Showalter's introduction to the Penguin edition of *Mrs. Dalloway* opened many enlightening perspectives. For insights into the text and its meaning, I am especially indebted to Stuart N. Clarke, Anne Fernald, and Mark Hussey. The many scholars and critics whose work I had gratefully in mind while writing this book include Elizabeth Abel, Ramathi Bandaranayake, Gillian Beer, Julia Briggs, Maria DiBattista, Christine Froula, Victoria Glendinning, Molly

Hite, Emily Kopley, Karen Levenback, Laurie Patton, Kathryn Simpson, Francesca Wade, Rebecca Walkowitz, Helen Wussow, and Alex Zwerdling. The far-flung members of the Virginia Woolf Mailing List offered welcome gifts of knowledge and interpretation.

The credit for some of the points I make in this book belongs to people whose names I never knew or can't remember: questioners in lecture audiences, participants in classroom discussions. I was struck a few years ago by a critic's phrase, "Clarissa's triumph in the little room," and wanted to praise its author; but I no longer know where I saw it, and online sources haven't found it.

A critic ought to write for readers more intelligent than he is. In this book, as always, I have written for Cheryl Mendelson, for the memory of Sir Frank Kermode, and for the memory of Elisabeth Sifton.

Most of what I know about the themes of this book I learned from Virginia Woolf, W. H. Auden, and the scholar, teacher, and friend to whom it is dedicated.

REFERENCE NOTES

The texts of Virginia Woolf's novels are easily available online in searchable texts—the best is an impressively accurate edition, *The Complete Works of Virginia Woolf*, compiled by someone who uses the lowercase pseudonym "pynch"—so I have not provided page references to any specific edition. As I noted in my preface, scanned images of the early editions of *Mrs. Dalloway*, and texts derived from each, may be found at https://mendelson.org/VirginiaWoolf. The following notes identify by date quotations from Virginia Woolf's diary and letters; these are easily found in standard printed and online editions. Publication details are also provided for works by other authors.

ix   *I want to give life and death*   Diary, 19 June 1923

1   *Genius it has*   Diary, 6 September 1922

2   *a similarity to Dante's Comedy*   Erich Auerbach, *Mimesis* (translated by Willard R. Trask, 1953), 547

3   T. S. Eliot, "*Ulysses*, Order, and Myth," *The Dial*, November 1923; *Selected Prose of T. S. Eliot*, edited by Frank Kermode (1975), 177

9   *this soul, or life within us*   "Montaigne," *Times Literary Supplement*, 31 January 1924; *The Common Reader: First Series* (1925)

10   *my discovery; how I dig*   Diary, 30 August 1923

21 *What she felt* W. H. Auden, "A Consciousness of Reality," *New Yorker*, 6 March 1964; *Forewords and Afterwords* (1973)
22 *that in some vague way* Letter to Goldsworthy Lowes Dickinson, 27 October 1931
23 *washing my hands* Diary, 2 June 1921
28 *war-neurosis* W. H. R. Rivers, *Instinct and the Unconscious* (1922), 205; *far more bearable*, 201
29 *care more particularly* William Osler, "Address to the students of the Albany Medical College, 1899," *Albany Medical Annals*, 1899, 308
30 *must always* listen *to* Oliver Sacks, *Migraine* (1970), 254 (without italics in the 1993 edition, 252)
32 *It was a subject that* Letter to Gwen Raverat, 1 May 1925
33 *I meet somebody* Letter to Stella Benson, 12 January 1933, *Congenial Spirits*, edited by Joanne Trautman Banks (1989)
34 *In such cases* Rivers, *Instinct and the Unconscious*, 200
35 *if every one* Auden, "Sigmund Freud," *New Republic*, 6 October 1952; *Prose, Vol. III (1949–1955)* (2008), 343
35 *gulping up Freud* Diary, 8 December 1939
35 *I suppose that I did* "A Sketch of the Past," *Moments of Being* (2nd ed., 1985), 93
48 *thinking that the birds* "Old Bloomsbury," *Moments of Being* (2nd ed., 1985), 45
56 *It took me a year's groping* Diary, 15 October 1923
65 *London is enchanting* Diary, 5 May 1924
65 *the civilization that has escaped* E. M. Forster, *A Passage to India* (1924), chapter 32
66 *without a cement of blood* Auden, "Vespers" (from "Horae Canonicae")
67 *many a sore bottom* Auden, "Prospero" (from "The Sea and the Mirror")
71 *L. and I quarrelled* Diary, 9 May 1926
71 *the practice of art* "Why Art To-Day Follows Politics," *Daily Worker*, 14 December 1936
72 *the women would cease* "Memories of a Working Women's Guild," *Yale Review*, September 1930
78 *the imperial idea* "Thunder at Wembley," *Nation & Athenaeum*, 28 June 1924
81 *Americans always want* Auden, letter to James Yates, 16 June 1939; quoted in Edward Mendelson, *Early Auden, Later Auden* (2017), 382

REFERENCE NOTES ☙ 133

86 *real people* "An Essay in Criticism" [on Hemingway], *New York Herald Tribune*, 9 October 1927
97 *something new and elemental* Auerbach, *Mimesis*, 552
99 *The aim of its eros* Auden, *The Age of Anxiety* (1947), Part III
117 *word-coining power* Diary, 13 April 1930
120 *very charming* Diary, 8 October 1922
121 *I meant* nothing Letter to Roger Fry, 27 May 1927
122 *I want to give a picture* Reported in Frank Budgen, *James Joyce and the Making of* Ulysses (1934), chapter 4

INDEX

Aeneid (Virgil), 16
archetypes, 12–15, 22
Auden, W. H., 21, 35, 49, 53n, 66, 67, 81, 95, 99, 117
Auerbach, Erich, 1–2, 97–98
Augustine, 26, 84n
Avatar (film), 69

Balzac, Honoré de, 17–18
Beckett, Samuel, 124
Bexborough, Lady, 37, 44, 77, 109
Bradshaw, Lady, 28, 50, 52, 61, 63, 73, 74, 126
Bradshaw, Sir William: goddesses of, 27, 31, 40, 51, 62–64, 68–69, 71n, 90; methods of, 8, 25–33, 38, 50; power of, 5, 10, 19, 40–42, 58n, 61–64, 66, 73–74, 76, 78, 84, 89–90, 116, 126
Bradshaw, David, 45n, 107–108, 123
Brontë, Charlotte, 6–8
Bruton, Lady Millicent, x, 19, 44–45, 50–54, 61–62, 66, 68–69, 73, 76, 116

Daily Worker, The, 71
Daisy, 83–84, 100
Dalloway, Richard: as husband, x, 8n, 11, 19, 73, 75, 78, 82–83, 87, 89, 92, 99–100, 111, 116, 126; as Member of Parliament, 28, 33, 36, 42, 45, 53–54, 72
Dalloway, Elizabeth, 3, 19, 66–68, 76, 89–90, 94, 98, 107, 126
Dante, 1–2, 16
Dickens, Charles, 17–18
Dostoyevsky, Fyodor, 6, 9

Eagleton, Terry, 2n
Eliot, T. S., 3–4, 10n, 117
empire, 51–79. *See also* India
Emre, Merve, 111–112
Evans (Army officer), 38–39, 47

Fernald, Anne, 108, 111, 115, 117, 123
Fields, Barbara J., 96n
flowers, x, 84
Forster, E. M., 65, 127n
Frankenstein (Mary Shelley), 6, 92n

Frazer, Sir James, 10n
Freud, Sigmund, 34–36

Gordon, General George, 60–61
Grass, Günter, 70n

Henderson, Ellie, 75, 78, 126
Hogarth Press, ix, xi, 4, 35, 105–107, 117
Holmes, Dr., 32, 37, 40–42, 45, 64

India, 11, 50, 51–52, 59–65, 74, 76, 82–83, 100, 119

Jane Eyre (Charlotte Brontë), 6–8
Joyce, James, 1, 3–4, 8, 69, 123n

Kilman, Doris, x, 19, 45, 62–68, 73, 76, 89–90, 94, 98, 126

love, 11, 23, 36, 38, 39, 81–105, 109. *See also* sex

Maxse, Kitty, 120–121
McNichol, Stella, xi, 107, 108n, 114, 123
medicine, 25–50. *See also* Bradshaw, Sir William
Montaigne, Michel de, 9, 46–47, 87

Odyssey (Homer), 1, 3–5, 11–13, 15, 122
Osler, Sir William, 29

Parry, Helena, 23, 128
Parry, Sylvia, 43, 49, 88

Parry, Justin, 36n, 43
Passage to India, A (E. M. Forster), 65
Poe, Edgar Allan, 18
politics, 50, 51–52, 66, 69, 70–73, 78, 92

Raverat, Jacques, 77n, 106, 125
religion, 9, 19, 67, 88–90
Rivers, W. H. R., 28–29, 34, 40–41, 46

Sacks, Oliver, 30
Said, Edward, 2n
Seton, Sally, 24, 36, 43n, 49, 68n, 77, 79, 84, 90n, 94, 96, 98–101, 103, 110, 113, 116, 125–126; as Lady Rosseter, 100
sex, 11, 18, 26, 39, 43, 61, 81n, 83, 87, 90–92, 93n, 94–95, 99, 100–102. 119
Shakespeare, William, xi, 62n, 68n, 112–113, 123
Shelley, Mary, 92
Showalter, Elaine, 107
siblings, x, 43, 67
Smith, Zadie, 100n
Spengler, Oswald, 21

Ulysses (Joyce), 1, 3, 20–21, 69, 122, 123n

Walsh, Peter: and Clarissa, 3, 10–16, 19, 23, 26n, 30, 33, 36–37, 43–44, 48–49, 54, 57, 73, 77–79, 87–88, 90–92, 94n, 95–96,

98–101, 103, 107, 110–111, 113–116, 120–122; and India, 59–65, 82–85
Warren Smith, Septimus, 5, 7–10, 15–24, 32–50, 62–68, 76, 100–103, 107n, 109, 111, 112n, 115n, 116n, 117n
Warren Smith, Lucrezia, 18, 25, 28–29, 31, 39–41, 48, 62, 100, 116, 117n, 122
Whitbread, Hugh, x, 19, 32, 44, 51, 53–54, 57
Woolf, Leonard, ix, xi, 33, 43n, 71, 92
Woolf, Virginia, other works by: *Between the Acts*, 23, 30, 72n, 122n; The Diary of Virginia Woolf, 43n, 56, 70n, 70–71, 92, 105; "An Essay in Criticism," 86–87, 133; *The Hours* (early title of *Mrs. Dalloway*), 1, 3, 118; *Jacob's Room*, 102n, 124n; "Mr. Bennett and Mrs. Brown," 3, 22; "Mrs. Dalloway in Bond Street," 37, 46n, 124n; *Night and Day*, 54n; "Old Bloomsbury," 48; *Orlando*, 86n, 96–97; *A Room of One's Own*, 6–7, 70n, 73; "The Symbol," 30; *Three Guineas*, 70n, 73; "Thunder at Wembley," 78–79, 132; *To the Lighthouse*, 1–3, 31–32, 35–36, 74, 81n, 121; *The Voyage Out*, 31; *The Waves*, 5n, 22, 23, 30, 34n, 43n, 110; "Why Art To-Day Follows Politics," 71, 132; *The Years*, 70
Wright, G. Patton, 107, 108n, 111n, 114, 124n
Wussow, Helen, 118n

GPSR Authorized Representative: Easy Access System Europe, Mustamäe tee
50, 10621 Tallinn, Estonia, gpsr.requests@easproject.com

www.ingramcontent.com/pod-product-compliance
Lightning Source LLC
Chambersburg PA
CBHW022017290426
44109CB00015B/1201